THE
HIDDEN
HUT

THE
HIDDEN
HUT

SIMON STALLARD

HarperCollins*Publishers*

It's a brisk April evening on the Roseland Peninsula, Cornwall. In a small sheltered cove, storm lanterns flicker as a bobble-hatted crowd clad in Gor-Tex and goose-down huddle together. Friends and families sit shoulder to shoulder with strangers on long, weathered tables. Hot-water bottles are stowed inside coats and wines are shared generously. Behind, a team of chefs tend to steaming pans over wood fires as a local fishing crew deliver their last catch of the day. Spirits are high and the atmosphere is alive with anticipation.

The reason for the gathering? It's 'feast night' at the Hidden Hut.

Introduction

I remember it wasn't the easiest of conversations, persuading my partner Jem that we should give up our jobs and take on the lease of an old wooden shed on the coast path. The country at the time was in the midst of an economic downturn, restaurants were being hit hard and we'd not long signed the mortgage of our first house. Only something really special could have drawn us to take such a risk.

Having trained and worked as chef since I was 16, my career had taken me all over the world, from New York and New Delhi to the fish markets of Newlyn. Cornwall was now my home and I felt it was a truly exciting place to be a chef. The region is flush with some of the most desirable produce in the country. Its frost-free climate allows for a longer growing season and beautifully ripe fruits. The seas are clean and plentiful, and the fields are lush with rich pasture. Large intensive farms are a rarity down here. It's mainly small-scale, traditional production. Everything feels slightly slower and a little less refined, and that is just what I love.

I used to walk past the little green shed every morning on my way to work. At the time, it was used as a kiosk for selling lollies and plastic beach toys. It had a retro charm to it, but it was only open during the summer holidays. For the other ten months of the year it was closed and boarded up. I would watch the cattle grazing in the pastures above and the fishing boats harvesting the seas below; it encompassed everything I loved about Cornwall. There was something special there that moved me. However, the hut had been leased from the National Trust by the same family for over 25 years and I was told there was no way they would be letting it go. It had to remain a pipe dream.

However, three years later, I heard some news from a very reliable source in our local, the Plume of Feathers. The National Trust was accepting tenders for the hut from interested parties. I literally grabbed my coat and came straight home to Jem to let her know. Our proposal was sent off to Lanhydrock House the next morning. As the only people who'd shown an interest, it wasn't long before the lease was signed and our journey had begun.

But it wasn't all plain sailing. I remember the February morning I picked up the keys and trekked over the cliffs to take a proper look at our new venture. The mud track that was meant for deliveries had been eroded into a stream, leaving the place only accessible by foot, and in wellies at that. As I tried to work out which key went where, I realised the locks had frozen tight in the salty air, so I had to break in through the hatches. Huge spiders the size of my hand scuttled away as I clambered over the counter into the dusty, derelict shed. The view from it was breathtaking and there was so much potential, but Porthcurnick Beach was no Padstow or St Ives. This was remote, deepest, undiscovered Cornwall. There was not a soul to be seen as far as the eye could see. What on earth had we taken on?

It took ten long weeks of hard graft to renovate the hut. Being in such an unspoilt, natural setting, we couldn't add anything of any permanence. We built an outdoor kitchen that could be dismantled and removed at the end of each season and installed long tables in the sand made from a fallen tree. What seemed like an impossible feat only added to the magic of it. We were finally ready to open.

To create the daily menu, I struck up deals with local fishermen, farmers and growers. Having worked at the local fish markets, I knew what to buy, and when. If they had a huge glut of, say, mackerel, we would take a load at a good price and set up a couple of grills on the clifftop. We'd put a blackboard up on the road and a post on Facebook, and just hope enough people would see it and drop by. It was simple but it worked well. We would always be busy on those days and I loved people's enthusiasm for this type of offering. But it soon became apparent it wasn't sustainable. It wasn't long before too many people would turn up hoping for the blackboard menu and we couldn't feed them all. There was nothing worse than people trekking over only for them to leave hungry. We needed to adapt our tactics.

We decided to move these events to the evenings when the coast was quieter and, because we didn't have a phone line, we sold tickets online as the method of booking. They became known as 'feast nights' and they were the offering I had been dreaming about all these years. We cooked one dish over a wood fire, showcasing just a few key ingredients delivered direct from the fields and boats. Anything from slow-roasted lamb to huge steaming pans of seafood paella over fire pits. There was no choice and all the food was served at once, straight from the grill; but it was the freshest food you could wish for. All the usual dining luxuries such as waiter service, wine menus, even plates and cutlery, were pared down – we just provided the food and setting, and let people make the nights their own. As only one dish was cooked per evening, we had a calendar rather than a menu; it certainly wasn't a normal way of running a restaurant service, but it felt right for this place.

Eight years and 64 firewood deliveries later, we have created something I am so proud to be a part of. The shed became the Hidden Hut and our feast nights the fastest-selling ticketed

food events in the UK. Despite no formal advertising – not even a signpost on the footpath – people stumbled across us and shared their discoveries by word of mouth. It wasn't long before it took off on social media and then the mainstream media were spreading our story, too.

Today, the Hidden Hut has become a food destination in its own right. It's been filmed for ITV and the BBC and has been featured in almost every major publication from *Vogue* and *Bon Appétit* to the *Observer* in its Top 40 Best Restaurants. It's developed its own coastal community. If you've picked up this book, it's likely you've already come across us and are part of the story. If you're new to us, then welcome! We are lucky that those who have sought us out over the years have tended to share our values and appreciate the simple, windswept pleasures our hut offers. This book of recipes is our way of saying of thank you.

13   Introduction

14   Introduction

15   Introduction

Cornwall enjoys the latest sunrise in the country. Dawn happens 'dreckly' here and that always feels quite appropriate.

For me, the ritual of cooking breakfast is about stopping and taking time, whether that's for a family sit-down or some solitude with the morning papers. It's not something most of us are able to do every day. It's more of a weekend/day-off affair. This chapter is for those mornings. A collection of long, laid-back breakfasts and brunches. It's all about picking great produce, putting on the coffee and getting into the holiday vibe.

1
Dawn

DOUGHNUTS AT DAWN

Small, freshly cooked doughnuts are great with a coffee. The batter gives you 20–25 golf-ball-sized doughnuts, so they are perfect for sharing. They are moreish, though – so they won't hang around for long. You could add some ground cinnamon to the sugar for dusting the doughnuts, if you liked.

Makes 20–25

1 vanilla pod
300ml whole milk, lukewarm (see Yeast Tip)
50g unsalted butter, melted and cooled to lukewarm
7g sachet active dried yeast
75g caster sugar, plus extra for coating
3 large eggs, lightly beaten
400g plain flour
1 tsp fine sea salt
sunflower oil, for deep-frying

Cut the vanilla pod in half lengthways and scrape out the seeds onto a plate. Pour the milk into a jug and add the butter, yeast, 1 teaspoon of the sugar and the vanilla seeds to create a vanilla-flavoured, yeasted milk. Stir well and leave for 5 minutes so that the yeast is activated. Beat in the eggs.

In a large mixing bowl, sift in 300g of the flour, the remaining sugar and the salt. Make a well in the centre and stir in the warm yeasted milk to create a lump-free batter. Cover the bowl with a clean tea towel or cling film and leave the batter to rise in a warm place for 1½ hours or until doubled in size.

Fill a deep-fryer or a large heavy-based saucepan one-third full with oil and heat it to 170°C (test by frying a small cube of bread; it should brown in 40 seconds). Using two soup spoons, spoon the wet batter into balls and gently drop them into the oil. Cook for 3 minutes, watching carefully and rolling them in the oil so that they brown evenly all over. Cook the doughnuts in batches of 4–5 so that you don't overfill the pan and cool the oil down too much.

Once they are done, remove them from the oil using a slotted spoon. To check that they are ready, cut one in half to make sure the dough is cooked through and not wet in the middle. Drain on a kitchen paper-lined plate, then dust with sugar and eat while they are still warm.

Yeast tip
Make sure the milk is no hotter than lukewarm or it might kill the yeast.

19   Dawn

SPICED FLASK OATS

There is something to be said for getting up in time to enjoy the sunrise. They are a magical few minutes of the day and totally worth getting out of bed for.

But you're probably not quite ready for breakfast yet? Make yourself a warming flask of chai porridge and take it out with you. When you're ready, crack open the lid and enjoy being greeted by the fragrant milky steam. It's the perfect fuel for a coastal walk.

Serves 1

350ml whole milk
2 cloves
1 star anise
1 cinnamon stick
zest of 1 orange
1 tbsp caster sugar
50g rolled porridge
    oats

Pour the milk into a small heavy-based saucepan and add the spices, orange zest and sugar. Bring to the boil over a medium-high heat, then reduce the heat and simmer for 2 minutes. Turn off the heat and leave the spices in the milk to infuse for 10 minutes.

Strain to remove the whole spices. Return the pan to the hob, add the oats and simmer for 3–6 minutes, depending on the coarseness of the oats, stirring continously. Pour into a vacuum flask with a cup lid, grab a spoon and consume on a clifftop (or the train on your morning commute).

21   Dawn

APRICOT, HONEY AND ROSEMARY MUFFINS

This recipe makes enough batter for 12 muffins. The batter freezes brilliantly, so you can enjoy freshly baked muffins for many mornings after you've made the mix. Just put the batter into the muffin cases and freeze them, then pull out as many as you need the night before to defrost and cook to enjoy them fresh in the morning.

When making the mix, keep the apricots and pecan nuts quite chunky to give the muffins some bite.

Makes 12

350g plain flour
2 tsp baking powder
a large pinch of sea salt
2 tbsp finely chopped
    rosemary leaves, plus
    12 small rosemary sprigs
120g pecan nuts,
    roughly chopped
120g dried apricots,
    roughly chopped
2 large eggs
125g golden caster sugar
125g unsalted
    butter, melted
240ml buttermilk
100g honey

Preheat the oven to 200°C (180°C fan oven) gas mark 6 and line a 12-cup muffin tray with 12 tulip muffin cases. Sift the flour, baking powder and salt into a large mixing bowl and add the chopped rosemary, pecan nuts and apricots.

In a separate bowl, whisk together the eggs and sugar until light and creamy, then whisk in the melted butter, buttermilk and honey until well combined. Pour this mixture into the dry ingredients and fold everything together using a spatula until just combined. Be careful not to work the mixture too much or the muffins will be tough – it doesn't matter if it is still slightly lumpy.

Spoon the batter evenly into the cake cases. Top each one with a sprig of rosemary to decorate. Bake the muffins for 25–30 minutes until risen and golden and a skewer inserted into the middle of a muffin comes out clean. Transfer to a wire rack. Serve warm or cold.

SMOKEY BACON PASTRIES

Crispy dry-cured smoked bacon, rich yolky eggs and Cornish Brie make for a great breakfast pastry filling. I like to enjoy these with a bit of cranberry relish on the side.

Makes 12

butter, for greasing
500g puff pastry,
    defrosted if frozen
plain flour, for dusting
8 rashers of streaky
    smoked bacon
6 spring onions,
    thinly sliced
50ml double cream
3 large eggs
50g Parmesan
    cheese, grated
180g Cornish Brie, diced
freshly ground black
    pepper
cranberry relish, to serve

Preheat the oven to 220°C (200°C fan oven) gas mark 7 and grease a 12-cup muffin tray with butter. Roll out the puff pastry on a lightly floured work surface. To make it extra flaky, fold it in half and roll it out again. Do this twice more, then roll it out thinly one final time.

Take a 12cm round pastry cutter and check that you can get 12 circles out of the pastry before you start to cut them, as you don't want to have to re-roll the pastry. Roll it out a bit more if needed. Cut out the pastry discs and use them to line the 12 holes of the muffin tray, then put it to one side.

Grill the bacon until crispy and golden, then shred into small pieces. Divide the bacon bits evenly between the pastry cases, followed by the spring onions.

In a large bowl, whisk the cream to soft peaks. In a separate bowl, whisk the eggs until light and fluffy, then fold them into the cream. Season with black pepper and fold in the Parmesan.

Pour the filling into the pastry cases and top with the diced Brie, dividing it evenly between the tartlets. Bake for 20 minutes, turning the oven temperature down to 200°C (180°C fan oven) gas mark 6 after 10 minutes, until golden on top and the pastry is cooked through. Make sure the pastries are cooked and move freely in the muffin tray before taking them out of the oven. Serve warm or cold with cranberry relish on the side.

BUTTERMILK DROP CAKES WITH LEMON CURD

Serves 4

Topped with warm lemon curd and served straight from the stove, these drop cakes are a sure-fire way to draw everyone to the breakfast table. Serve with berries and crème fraîche.

320g plain flour
1 tsp baking powder
a good pinch of sea salt
50g caster sugar
2 large eggs
290ml buttermilk
60g butter, plus extra
   for frying
crème fraîche and
   berries, to serve

FOR THE LEMON CURD
90g butter, cubed
140g caster sugar
a pinch of sea salt
120ml lemon juice
   (about 3 lemons)
3 large egg yolks
1 large egg

FOR THE MINT SUGAR
4 tbsp caster sugar
a good handful of
   mint leaves

First, make the lemon curd. Put the butter in a heatproof bowl over a saucepan of gently simmering water, making sure the base of the bowl doesn't touch the water. Add the sugar, salt and lemon juice. Stir until well combined and the butter has melted. Remove the bowl from the heat and set to one side.

In a separate bowl, whisk together the egg yolks and egg. Add this to the lemon and butter mixture and whisk to combine. Return the bowl to the simmering saucepan and heat for 10 minutes or until the mixture thickens. Remove from the heat and leave to cool a little.

To make the mint sugar, simply either blitz the sugar and mint leaves in a food processor or bash them together using a mortar and pestle. Put to one side.

Preheat the oven to 110°C (90°C fan oven) gas mark ¼. Sift the flour, baking powder and salt into a large mixing bowl and stir in the sugar. Add the eggs and buttermilk, and whisk everything together to make a smooth batter.

Put half the butter in a non-stick frying pan and melt it over a medium-low heat. Mix the melted butter into the batter.

Put the frying pan back over the heat and add tablespoonfuls of the mixture in small pools around the pan – you should be able to do 4–5 at a time. Cook for 1 minute on the first side, or until bubbles form on the surface. Flip them over and cook for 1 minute.

Remove from the pan and keep warm on a plate wrapped up in a tea towel in the oven while you cook the remaining batter in the same way, adding a little more of the remaining butter to the pan each time.

Serve the drop cakes warm, drizzled with lemon curd, some crème fraîche and fresh berries and a sprinkle of mint sugar.

Roasted
Figs with
Honey and
Ricotta on
Walnut
Toast

Roasted Figs with Honey and Ricotta on Walnut Toast

Hot walnut toast with whipped cinnamon butter served with roasted figs, ricotta, flaked almonds (crushed pistachios also work really well) and honey. You can make the loaf and cinnamon butter the day before, if you wish. Your kitchen will smell like a Danish bakery!

Serves 8–10

750g spelt flour
2 tsp sea salt
1½ tsp active dried yeast
3 rounded tsp honey
2 tbsp walnut oil
40g walnuts, chopped
oil, for greasing

FOR THE WHIPPED
CINNAMON BUTTER
170g butter, softened
45g soft dark brown sugar
2½ tsp ground cinnamon

FOR THE ROASTED FIGS
50g butter
5 star anise
10 large, ripe figs, halved

TO SERVE
50g flaked almonds
honey, for drizzling
ricotta cheese
lemon zest

First, make the walnut loaf. You'll need to start at least 3 hours before serving, or make it the night before. In a large bowl, mix together the flour, salt and yeast. Add the honey and 450ml warm water, and give it a good stir until it begins to come together. Add the oil and knead for 10 minutes or until soft and supple. Cover the dough in the bowl with a damp tea towel or cling film and leave it to rise in a warm place for 1 hour or until it doubles in size.

Once doubled in size, it's time to do a bit more kneading. This time you want to incorporate the walnuts. Keep going until the walnuts have become part of the dough. Grease a baking tray and form the dough into a loaf shape, then leave it to rest on the tray for 20 minutes. Preheat the oven to 220°C (200°C fan oven) gas mark 7.

Bake the loaf on the top shelf of the oven for 35 minutes or until it sounds hollow when tapped underneath. If it makes a dent when tapped, it's not quite done. Leave it to cool on a wire rack for at least 10 minutes before slicing.

To make the cinnamon butter, beat all the ingredients together until fluffy. Roll in greaseproof paper and form into a sausage, then chill in the fridge until needed. Allow the butter to come to room temperature before serving (this will enhance the cinnamon flavour).

For the roasted figs, preheat the oven to 240°C (220°C fan oven) gas mark 9. Melt the butter in a heavy-based saucepan over a medium heat, and allow it to foam. Add the star anise and cook over a low heat for 10–15 minutes until the anise flavours the butter.

Put the figs, cut side up, on a baking tray and drizzle over the star anise butter. Roast for 15–20 minutes until the figs are tender.

Slice the bread and toast it, then spread the hot toast with the cinnamon butter. Top with the figs, sprinkle with flaked almonds and serve with honey, ricotta and a sprinkling of lemon zest.

GRILLED MACKEREL WITH A WARM CORNISH SPLIT AND HORSERADISH SOURED CREAM

We serve these filled splits during the annual Portscatho Fish Festival. The mackerel comes in straight from the boats and onto our big wood-fired grills on the harbour jetty. Try to use the freshest possible mackerel. If you can, choose mackerel that are whole so that you can check if the eyes are clear and bright. Then ask the fishmonger to fillet and pin-bone them for you, leaving the skin on.

Splits are like a proven scone. They are well worth the effort, especially when served warm from the oven. The subtle sweetness of the split and the punch from the horseradish really complement the oily mackerel. If you have a sweet tooth, try a bit of gooseberry jam in there too; it might just make your day.

Serves 6

12 mackerel fillets, about 100g each, boned (see page 55), with skin
sunflower oil, for frying
100g watercress
sea salt and freshly ground black pepper
gooseberry jam (optional), to serve

FOR THE SPLITS
10g active dried yeast
1 rounded tsp caster sugar
200ml whole milk, lukewarm
265g strong white bread flour, plus extra for dusting

To make the splits, put the yeast in a bowl and mix in the sugar and milk. Leave to stand for 5 minutes to allow the yeast to activate.

Sift the bread flour and plain flour, and the salt, into a large mixing bowl, then rub the butter into the flour mix using your fingertips. Make a well in the centre, add the yeasty milk and mix to form a dough. Tip onto a floured work surface and knead for 10 minutes. Put in a clean bowl, cover with a damp tea towel or cling film and leave in a warm place to rise for 1 hour or until doubled in size.

Remove the dough from the bowl, knead again for 2 minutes, then shape into 6 rolls. Put these on a greased baking sheet. Brush with the egg yolk and sprinkle over a little grated horseradish. Leave to rise again in a warm place for 45 minutes. Preheat the oven to 200°C (180°C fan oven) gas mark 6.

100g plain flour
1 tsp fine sea salt
60g unsalted butter,
   softened, plus extra
   for greasing
1 egg yolk, lightly beaten
a little peeled and grated
   fresh horseradish

**FOR THE HORSERADISH
SOURED CREAM**
4 tbsp soured cream
30g peeled and grated
   fresh horseradish
2 tbsp lemon juice
1 tsp sea salt
½ tsp freshly ground
   black pepper

Bake the rolls for 25–30 minutes until light golden – to test they are cooked, tap the bottom of one of the rolls; it should sound hollow when ready. Cool slightly on a wire rack.

To make the horseradish soured cream, mix all the ingredients together a bowl.

Heat a non-stick frying pan over a medium-high heat. Season the mackerel well with salt and pepper. Heat 2 tablespoons of oil in the frying pan and add the fillets skin-side down – cook in batches of 2–4 fillets, depending on the size of your pan. Press down for the first 10 seconds so that the mackerel doesn't curl up. Cook for 2 minutes until crispy, then flip over and cook for a further 30 seconds on the other side. Repeat with the remaining fillets.

To serve, cut the warm splits horizontally like a burger bun, put two mackerel fillets in each bun along with a good spoonful of the horseradish soured cream and some watercress. If you have any gooseberry jam in the fridge, pop this out on the table, too, to add to the mackerel.

FLUFFIEST SMOKED HADDOCK OMELETTE

Serves 4

This is no ordinary omelette. Light, fluffy and delicately smokey, the yolks added towards the end give it a beautiful self-saucing finish when cut into.

300g skinless, boneless smoked haddock fillet
10 eggs
100ml double cream
8 spring onions, finely chopped
a small bunch of coriander, leaves chopped
1 tbsp olive oil
50g Cheddar cheese, finely grated
sea salt (if needed) and freshly ground black pepper

Put the haddock in a bowl and pour hot water from the kettle over it, then leave it to poach for 2 minutes. Drain and flake the fish into large chunks.

Separate four of the eggs, leaving the yolks in the shells for now. Put the whites in a clean, grease-free bowl and whisk them using an electric hand whisk until firm peaks form.

In a separate large bowl, whisk the remaining six whole eggs with the cream and season with pepper (you probably won't need much salt, if any, as the haddock is quite salty). Fold the egg whites into the egg and cream mixture, being careful not to knock out too much of the air. Using a spatula, quickly fold in the flaked haddock, spring onions and coriander.

Preheat the grill to high. Heat the oil in a frying pan with a heatproof handle over a medium heat. Pour the egg mix into the pan and use a spatula to move the mix around a bit so that it starts to cook evenly. Pop a lid on and leave to cook for 5 minutes in the pan or until well set on the bottom.

Remove the pan from the heat and gently tip the four egg yolks from their shells onto the top of the omelette. Sprinkle the top with the cheese and put the pan under the grill for 3–4 minutes until the omelette is turning golden on top and is cooked throughout, but the egg yolks are still runny. Serve immediately.

TOPPED CORNISH POTATO CAKES

Cornish potato cakes stacked up with sausage patties, blistered tomatoes and crispy potato skins. By popping a few baking potatoes into the oven first thing, you're well on the way to making a cooked brunch that will set you up for the day.

Serves 4

4 baking potatoes,
about 200g each
480g of your favourite
sausages
olive oil, for brushing
and shallow-frying
1 tsp flaked sea salt
40g butter, melted
10g plain flour, for dusting
sea salt and freshly
ground black pepper
basil leaves, to garnish

**FOR THE BLISTERED
TOMATOES**
400g cherry tomatoes,
sliced in half
4 spring onions,
finely shredded
a squeeze of lemon juice
1 tbsp olive oil
1 tsp nigella (black onion)
seeds

First thing in the morning, put the potatoes into the oven, set it for 200°C (180°C fan oven) gas mark 6 and leave to bake for 1–1½ hours or until soft. Cut each potato in half and scoop out the flesh into a bowl, keeping the skins. Leave until ready to use.

Preheat the oven to 190°C (170°C fan oven) gas mark 5. Remove the skins from the sausages and form the sausagemeat into eight small patties. Put to one side.

Thoroughly scrape off any remaining mash from the potato skins and cut the skins into 2.5cm slices. Brush with olive oil and sprinkle with the flaked sea salt. Put onto a baking tray and cook in the oven for 10 minutes.

Meanwhile, mash the potato with a fork, then add the butter and season with salt and pepper. Mix well. Divide the mash into eight even balls and gently flatten the top and bottom of each slightly, then dust in the flour.

Heat the olive oil for shallow-frying in a frying pan over a medium-high heat and pan-fry the balls for 1 minute on each side or until browned. Set these on a baking sheet and cook in the oven for 8 minutes.

Give your frying pan a quick clean, then fry the sausage patties in olive oil for 2 minutes on each side or until golden and crispy. Turn the oven right down to 110°C (90°C fan oven) gas mark ¼ and pop the patties in with the potato cakes to keep warm.

For the tomatoes, turn up the heat under the frying pan and cook the tomatoes for 2 minutes, turning once. Try not to stir them too much. Throw in the spring onions and add the lemon juice, oil and nigella seeds. Cook for 1 minute or so to lightly wilt the onions.

Serve the potato cakes topped with the sausage patties. Spoon oven the tomatoes and spring onions, and top with the crispy potato skins and some fresh basil leaves.

CHILLI SAFFRON TOAST
WITH CRISPY BACON

Here's one for chilli lovers. Head down to your local bakery to pick up a Cornish saffron loaf, and get the frying pan on for this eggy bread with a twist. The fiery green chilli and coriander really wake everything up. These toasts are great with a bowl of Greek yogurt on the side.

Serves 4

2 large eggs, beaten
16 rashers of smoked
    streaky bacon
40g butter
4 slices of 1 large saffron
    loaf, about 2.5cm
    thick and 100g each
4 tsp wild honey
1–2 small green finger
    chillies, to taste –
    depending on how
    hot you like it –
    finely chopped
a bunch of coriander, leaves
    roughly chopped
sea salt and freshly
    ground black pepper

Season the eggs with salt and pepper, then pour them into a deep saucer or shallow bowl and put to one side. This is for dipping the saffron bread into.

Preheat the oven to 195°C (175°C fan oven) gas mark 5½ and line a baking tray with baking parchment. Lay out the rashers of bacon on the prepared baking tray. Lay over a second layer of parchment on top of the bacon and put another baking tray on the top to keep the bacon flat and stop it curling up while it cooks. To get crispy bacon, cook in the oven for 15 minutes.

In the meantime, melt the butter in a frying pan over a medium heat. Dip each slice of saffron bread into the egg and press down to soak up the egg, then turn over so that both sides are soaked equally. Fry for 2 minutes on each side or until golden brown. When all the slices are fried, put them onto a baking tray and pop them in the oven with the bacon to keep hot until you're ready to serve.

Put the crispy bacon on top of the saffron toast and drizzle with honey. Serve sprinkled with the chillies and coriander.

Asparagus
Baked Eggs,
Potato Rösti
and Field
Mushrooms

Asparagus Baked Eggs, Potato Rösti and Field Mushrooms

For those fresh spring mornings when asparagus is in season and calling out for runny yolks. These asparagus baked eggs are served with golden rösti, richly flavoured field mushrooms and a citrusy tarragon hollandaise sauce for a really wholesome vegetarian breakfast.

Serves 8

300g Cornish asparagus, tough ends snapped off
50g butter
2 tbsp light olive oil
2 white onions, finely sliced
8 eggs
sea salt and freshly ground black pepper

FOR THE POTATO RÖSTI

2kg potatoes, peeled and coarsely grated
2 tsp fine sea salt
1 tsp freshly ground black pepper
100g butter

Preheat the oven to 170°C (150°C fan oven) gas mark 3. Chop the tips off the asparagus and put them to one side. Using a swivel vegetable peeler, pare the asparagus into ribbons.

Melt the butter with the oil in a large frying pan over a medium heat. Add the onions and a good pinch of salt and pepper, then cook for 8–10 minutes until lightly caramelised. Add the asparagus ribbons and cook for a further 1 minute.

In a small roasting tin, lay out two-thirds of the onion and asparagus mix, then crack the eggs over the top, leaving a gap between each one. Put the remaining onions and asparagus ribbons, and the asparagus tips, over the top to protect the eggs. Lightly season with salt and pepper and set aside.

To make the rösti, put the grated potato in large mixing bowl and add the salt and pepper. Melt the butter in a saucepan over a low heat. Pour the melted butter over the potato and mix well. Once well coated, split the mixture in half and press it into two non-stick frying pans. Cook over a medium heat for 4 minutes or until the edges start to become golden.

FOR THE TARRAGON HOLLANDAISE
250g butter
2 large egg yolks
1 tbsp white wine vinegar
juice of ¼ large lemon,
    or to taste
1 tbsp finely chopped
    tarragon leaves

FOR THE FIELD MUSHROOMS
2 tbsp light olive oil
8 field mushrooms, peeled
    and cut into 1cm slices
50g butter

Hold a chopping board or a plate over the frying pan and flip the pan over to turn the rösti out onto the board, then sweep the rösti back into the pan to cook the other side. Do the same with the other pan of rösti. Cook on this side for 2 minutes or until turning golden. Transfer the rösti from each pan to a baking tray.

Put the rösti, and the roasting tin with the asparagus mix, into the oven, and bake for 15 minutes or until the rösti is golden all over and the egg whites are set but the yolks are still runny.

While the rösti and asparagus are cooking, make the hollandaise. Put the butter in a saucepan over a medium-low heat and gently melt, then set aside. Put the egg yolks and vinegar in a heatproof bowl set over a saucepan of gently simmering water, making sure the base of the bowl doesn't touch the water, and whisk continuously until the eggs have thickened to the consistency of mayonnaise. If it becomes too thick, add a tiny splash of warm water.

Take off the heat and slowly whisk in the melted butter in a steady stream, discarding the white sediment at the bottom of the pan. Add 1 tablespoon of warm water, most of the lemon juice and all the tarragon, then season with salt and pepper and add more lemon if required.

To cook the mushrooms, heat the oil in a large saucepan over a medium heat and add the mushrooms and a good pinch of salt and pepper. Cook for 2 minutes, then add the butter and cook for 2 minutes more. Serve the asparagus baked eggs with the rösti, mushrooms and tarragon hollandaise.

Lunch is the main meal to be served from our beach kitchen. The menu is chalked up daily, often twice daily if it's busy, and we whizz through produce. Our food doesn't follow any particular cuisine; instead, we allow ourselves to be influenced by the seasons and the fresh produce they bring, and even by the variable weather. Cornish soul food might be a way to describe it.

When browsing the recipes for inspiration, let yourself be guided by the day around you. If it's a hot, sunny day, bring out the salads and grilled fish. If it's cold and blustery, warm up with spiced dhals and slow-cooked joints of lamb.

If you're interested in having a go at building your own wood grill or fire pit, there is a feature (see pages 70–79) that takes you through it step by step. Though I warn you: once you start cooking with fire, it can get pretty addictive!

Noon

Soup Sundays at the Hidden Hut

Come wind, rain or shine, a warming bowl of soup can solve everything.

Soup Sundays have become a bit of an institution at the Hidden Hut. The appeal of hugging a warm pot of soup after a long coastal walk is pretty unbeatable. The atmosphere on these days is great – everybody is in day-off mode in their wellies or walking boots. Dogs and children play on the beach. The super-brave even swim here from the village! The place becomes a hub where you end up bumping into old friends and meeting new ones.

Soup Sundays for us are all about the spring and autumn months when the temperature starts to dip and the best soup veggies are in season. We get up early in the morning and prep mountains of produce to make fresh stocks, adding flavours layer by layer. The night before, we roast chicken, simmer turbot frames (bones), braise oxtail and prove bread; everything is done from scratch. At noon we chalk up around five or six fresh soups onto the boards and offer them all for a fiver with bread, butter and a selection of toppings. For us, soups aren't an apologetic starter made from yesterday's leftovers; they are served as our main meal of the day on our busiest day of the week!

Humble and soul-warming, soup is a delicious treat at home, too. Just like at the hut, you can transform simple homemade soups into a more substantial offering with a selection of toppings – crispy onions, fried herbs, croutons, grated cheese, toasted seeds and nuts – whatever takes your fancy. Bread is important, too. If you can, go for an uncut fresh loaf or bake your own. If not, just toast what you've got topped with grilled cheese!

PUMPKIN GINGER SOUP WITH CHESTNUTS AND CRISPY FRIED SAGE

Serves 4–6

A warming autumnal soup – ideal for blustery days. It is great with a side of melted cheese on toast.

1kg peeled and deseeded pumpkin or butternut squash, cut into wedges
2 tbsp olive oil, plus extra for drizzling
1 tbsp honey
1 large white onion, diced
2 garlic cloves, finely chopped
30g piece of fresh root ginger, peeled and finely chopped
850ml vegetable stock
½ tsp freshly grated nutmeg
½ tsp ground cinnamon
sunflower oil, for shallow-frying
a few sage leaves
30ml double cream
100g peeled cooked chestnuts, roughly chopped
sea salt and freshly ground black pepper

Preheat the oven to 220°C (200°C fan oven) gas mark 7. Put the pumpkin in a roasting tin and drizzle with olive oil and the honey. Season with salt and pepper, and mix everything together well. Roast in the oven for 30–40 minutes until tender and caramelised.

While the pumpkin is roasting, heat the 2 tablespoons of olive oil in a large saucepan over a medium heat and sweat off the onion, garlic and ginger, until the onion is tender. Add the cooked pumpkin to the pan, along with the stock, nutmeg and cinnamon, bring to the boil, then reduce the heat and simmer everything together for 10 minutes.

Meanwhile, heat 1cm of sunflower oil in a small frying pan over a high heat. Flash-fry the sage for 30 seconds or until crispy, then drain on kitchen paper and sprinkle with salt.

Take the soup pan off the heat and stir in the cream. Blend the soup using a blender or food processor, then adjust the seasoning to taste. Serve the soup topped with the chestnuts and crispy sage leaves.

ROASTED SQUASH AND CAULIFLOWER DHAL

In the autumn, when the coastal path is swarming with hikers, veggie dhal absolutely flies out of our kitchen. If you swap the yogurt for a non-dairy alternative, you have yourself a tasty and substantial vegan lunch.

Serves 4

1 butternut squash, peeled, deseeded and cut into large chunks
1 cauliflower, cut into large florets
2 tbsp sunflower oil
2 tbsp coconut oil
1 tbsp mustard seeds
2 onions, diced
3 garlic cloves, finely chopped
50g piece of fresh root ginger, peeled and grated
2 green chillies, deseeded and finely chopped
1 tbsp ground cumin
1 tbsp ground coriander
1 tsp paprika
1 tsp ground turmeric
1 tbsp curry powder
2 tomatoes, deseeded and chopped
1 vegetable stock cube
400ml coconut milk
350g red lentils
1 tbsp caster sugar
juice of 2 lemons
1 tbsp garam masala
100g spinach
2 tbsp chopped coriander leaves
100g natural yogurt
4 spring onions, sliced
sea salt and freshly ground black pepper
toasted flatbreads, to serve

Preheat the oven to 220°C (200°C fan oven) gas mark 7. Put the squash and cauliflower in a roasting tin and add the sunflower oil, then season with salt and pepper. Toss to coat, then roast in the oven for 20 minutes. Put to one side.

Heat the coconut oil in a saucepan over a medium heat and fry the mustard seeds, onions, garlic, ginger and chillies for 5 minutes or until softened. Add the cumin, coriander, paprika, turmeric and curry powder, and cook for 1 minute.

Add the tomatoes to the pan and cook for 30 seconds, then crumble in the stock cube and add 1 litre water and the coconut milk. Bring to the boil. Add the lentils and cook over a medium heat for 20 minutes.

Add the sugar to the pan, followed by the lemon juice, garam masala, spinach, coriander and half the yogurt, then cook for a further 1 minute. Season with salt and pepper to taste.

Tip the roasted cauliflower and squash into the pan, stir then sprinkle over the spring onions and serve with the remaining yogurt and toasted flatbreads.

49   Noon

CHICKEN AND WILD GARLIC SOUP

Wild garlic is abundant in local woodlands. They are small ground-covering plants with broad leaves and a little cluster of white flowers during the spring, and they are often found alongside bluebells. If you come across any wild garlic when you are out and about, this recipe is a lovely way to make the best of it. This is an enriching dish full of the flavours of spring.

Homemade stock really is better made with the whole bird, so buy a whole chicken and joint it. Use the carcass and legs for this recipe and freeze the breasts (or use them in the Charred Chicken and Squash Salad on page 104). To make the soup more substantial, cook 200g dried rice noodles and put them in the bowl before adding the soup, if you like.

Serves 4–6

3 tbsp sunflower oil,
  plus extra for roasting
1 large chicken, jointed
  (you can ask your
  butcher to do this)
  and breasts reserved
  for another recipe
3 celery sticks,
  roughly diced
1 onion, roughly diced
1 leek, roughly chopped
1 large garlic bulb,
  cloves peeled
100g wild garlic leaves,
  roughly sliced (keep
  the flowers if you
  have them)
4 spring onions, finely
  sliced on the diagonal
a small handful of mint
  leaves, ripped
a small handful of coriander
  leaves, ripped
sea salt and freshly ground
  black pepper

Preheat the oven to 220°C (200°C fan oven) gas mark 7. Heat the sunflower oil in a large saucepan over a high heat and add the chicken legs, skin side down, along with the wings and the carcass (you may need to do this in batches, depending on the size of your pan). Fry over a very high heat, to brown all over. Transfer to a roasting tin and coat in a little more oil and a pinch of salt. Roast for 15–18 minutes until a deep golden brown.

Add the vegetables to the same pan (there should still be some oil in there) and put it back over a medium heat. Sweat the veg for 2 minutes or until starting to soften but not colour.

Once roasted, return the chicken to the pan and pour over 2 litres cold water. Season with salt and pepper. Bring to the boil, then reduce the heat and simmer for 1½ hours. Strain the soup and return the broth to the pan. Take the chicken from the sieve, remove the skin and shred the meat from the bones, discarding the bones and skin. Leave the meat to one side.

Divide the wild garlic among serving bowls and top with the spring onions. Divide the shredded chicken between the bowls and add the herbs.

Taste the broth and check for seasoning, adding more salt and pepper if needed. Ladle it over the chicken and greens in the bowl, and sprinkle over the garlic flowers, if you have them.

SWEET POTATO CHILLI BOWL

Serves 4–6

Perfect sustenance after a wintry coastal walk, the sweet potatoes and red lentils in this dish are lifted by the fresh herbs and chillies. It's a super-tasty veg soup.

700g sweet potatoes, peeled and diced into 2.5cm chunks
2 red onions, roughly chopped
4 garlic cloves, chopped
2 tbsp olive oil
100g red lentils
900ml vegetable stock
2 red chillies, deseeded and diced
200ml coconut cream
sea salt and freshly ground black pepper

TO SERVE
4 tbsp flaked almonds
a handful of coriander leaves, roughly chopped
a handful of mint leaves, roughly chopped
1 red chilli, deseeded and finely sliced
2 limes, quartered

Preheat the oven to 200°C (180°C fan oven) gas mark 6. Put the sweet potatoes on a baking tray and add the onions and garlic. Add the oil and toss to coat, then season with salt and pepper. Roast in the oven for 20 minutes.

Put the lentils in a heavy-based saucepan and add the stock and chillies. Bring to the boil, then reduce the heat and simmer for 20 minutes, then blend with a hand blender.

When the roasted vegetables are ready, add them to the lentil pan. Pour in the coconut cream, then return to the boil and simmer lightly for 15 minutes until the vegetables have broken down with the lentils.

Turn up the oven temperature to 220°C (200°C fan oven) gas mark 7 and put the flaked almonds on a baking tray. Toast them in the oven for 2–3 minutes, watching them carefully, until they just start to colour. Take them out and leave the tray one one side.

Serve in soup bowls topped with the fresh herbs, chilli slices, toasted almonds and lime quarters.

SALT COD AND TOMATO STEW
WITH SOURDOUGH TOASTS

Although salting cod sounds technical, it's so easy and can be done at home overnight. It makes the fish firmer and more versatile to use in dishes where unsalted cod would just disintegrate. It also intensifies the flavour. Tomato and salt cod is a classic combination.

Serves 4–6

350g fine sea salt
3 rosemary sprigs
350g cod fillet, skinned and pin-boned (see tip opposite)
2 tbsp olive oil
1 onion, diced
1 large carrot, diced
1 fennel bulb, diced
3 celery sticks, diced
125ml white wine
1 garlic clove, crushed
400g tin chopped tomatoes
800ml fish stock
¼ tsp smoked paprika
freshly ground black pepper
dill fronds and 4–6 tsp aioli (see page 90), to serve

FOR THE CROUTONS
10 slices of sourdough bread with crusts, cut into 1.5cm cubes
olive oil, for drizzling
sea salt

Start by salting the cod the day before. Put a good layer of the salt in the base of a shallow dish and add the rosemary. Lay the cod on top and sprinkle over the remaining salt, making sure the fish is completely covered. Cover with cling film and leave for 12 hours in the fridge. (Don't leave it for longer than this or you will need to soak the fish for longer when you come to use it.)

The next day, thoroughly rinse the salt from the cod. Put the cod in a large bowl and cover with plenty of fresh cold water, then leave it to soak for 10 minutes before draining. Preheat the oven to 220°C (200°C fan oven) gas mark 7.

Heat the oil in a large saucepan over a medium heat and cook the onion, carrot, fennel and celery. Add the wine and garlic, then simmer to reduce the liquid slightly. Add the tomatoes and bring to the boil. Pour in the stock and return to the boil, then reduce the heat and simmer for 20 minutes or until the vegetables are tender.

Stir in the paprika and season with pepper. Add the cod and leave it to cook and start to break up in the soup – this shouldn't take more than 2–3 minutes. Remove the pan from the heat and leave it to stand for 5 minutes.

Meanwhile, to make the croutons, spread out the bread on a baking tray. Drizzle with olive oil and a light sprinkling of salt. Put them in the hot oven and bake for 3 minutes. Remove from the oven and toss them so that they brown evenly. Return to the oven to bake for a further 3 minutes or until golden. Serve the soup with the croutons and dill fronds on top and a teaspoon of aioli per bowl.

Pin-boning

Tiny bones, known as pin bones, will spoil your experience of eating fish if they are left in. To remove them, use standard tweezers or special fish tweezers. First run your fingers over the fish to locate the bones, which are hidden just beneath the surface. They lie at an angle, so you'll need to grab the end with the tweezers and pull the bones upwards and sideways to remove them.

GREEN PEA SOUP WITH LEMON AND RICOTTA

Fresh peas are best in the late spring and early summer, though by using frozen peas this soup can be enjoyed at any time of the year. The recipe is very simple and takes less than 15 minutes to make.

Serves 4

750ml vegetable stock
700g fresh podded peas
　(or frozen peas)
4 tbsp ricotta cheese
zest of ½ lemon
75ml double cream
20g mint leaves, shredded
sea salt and freshly
　ground black pepper

Put the vegetable stock in a large saucepan over a high heat and bring it to a rolling boil, then add the peas. Simmer for 8–10 minutes, or until the peas are tender. (If using frozen peas, cook from frozen and simmer for about 5 minutes).

Meanwhile, mix the ricotta and lemon zest together in a small bowl.

Once the peas are cooked, remove the pan from the heat and stir in the cream and most of the mint leaves. Blend the soup in a blender or food processor, then season to taste with salt and pepper.

Divide the soup between four bowls and serve each topped with a tablespoon of the lemon ricotta and a few of the reserved mint leaves sprinkled over.

ST MAWES SMOKED HADDOCK CHOWDER

There is nearly always a pan of St Mawes Smoked Haddock Chowder cooking on the stove at the Hidden Hut, come rain or shine. More substantial than a soup, this chowder will serve up to six people with a good helping of bread on the side.

Serves 4–6

400g smoked haddock, with skin, pin-boned (see page 55)
1 bay leaf
1 litre whole milk
2 tbsp light olive oil
6 rashers of smoked streaky bacon, sliced
50g butter
2 onions, diced
3 celery sticks, diced
½ fennel bulb, diced
4 garlic cloves, crushed
50g plain flour
400g waxy potatoes, peeled and diced
300ml fish stock
165g tinned sweetcorn
3 tbsp chopped dill fronds
zest and juice of 1 lemon
sea salt and freshly ground black pepper
1 spring onion, finely chopped, to garnish

FOR THE CROUTONS
80g bread with crusts, cut into 1.5cm cubes
2 tbsp olive oil

Preheat the oven to 200°C (180°C fan oven) gas mark 6. First prepare the croutons. Spread out the bread on a baking tray. Drizzle with the olive oil and add a light sprinkling of salt. Bake for 3 minutes then remove from the oven and toss so that they brown evenly. Return to the oven for a further 3 minutes or until golden. Put to one side.

Now for the chowder. Put the haddock and bay leaf in a roasting tin and pour over the milk. Cover with foil and bake for 12 minutes. Discard the bay leaf, peel the skin from the haddock and flake the flesh into a bowl. Set aside and reserve the cooking milk.

Add the oil to a large saucepan over a medium-high heat and get it really hot. Fry the bacon until golden and crispy. Turn the heat down, add the butter and let it melt. Add the onions, celery, fennel and garlic, and sweat them in the butter until tender and translucent. Add the flour and cook for 2 minutes, stirring, to cook out the taste of the flour. Then, bit by bit, add the reserved cooking milk, stirring to make a thick sauce. Leave to cook over a very low heat.

Meanwhile, put the potatoes in a saucepan, add the fish stock and bring to the boil. Cook for 8 minutes, then transfer the potatoes and stock to the gently simmering chowder base.

Finally, add the smoked haddock, sweetcorn, dill and lemon zest and juice and season to taste. Cook for 2 minutes more to let the flavours combine. Garnish with the croutons and chopped spring onion, and serve immediately.

57   Noon

A Little Lobster Goes a Long Way

Lobsters are a luxury item and this is all about getting the most out of your catch or purchase. It is a way of serving four people a thoughtful two-course lunch using just two lobsters. Start with the summer vegetable cigars and tarragon dip, then finish with the velvety bisque and toasts.

Serves 4

2 live or cooked
   cold-water lobsters
sea salt and freshly
   ground black pepper

FOR THE LOBSTER BISQUE
2 tbsp olive oil
50g butter
4 celery sticks, sliced
5 garlic cloves, chopped
2 onions, chopped
½ fennel bulb, sliced
1 red chilli, deseeded
   and chopped
½ tsp coriander seeds
¼ tsp fennel seeds
1 star anise
2 tbsp tomato purée
100ml Pernod
300ml white wine
2 litres fish stock
2 bay leaves
zest of 1 lemon and juice
   of ½ lemon
50g tarragon sprigs
2 tbsp double cream

If you've caught your own lobsters or are buying live ones, you'll need to kill them before cooking. Put the live lobsters into the freezer for 30 minutes to sedate them. Once sedated, lie one flat, stomach side down, on a chopping board. Spike it firmly and quickly with a large sharp knife in the base of its head and swiftly cut straight down. Repeat with the other lobster. They are now ready to cook.

Fill a large saucepan with water and bring to the boil with a large pinch of salt. Once boiling, add the lobsters and set the timer to boil for 8 minutes. Remove the lobsters from the pan and refresh in iced water. Now continue with the preparation for cooked lobsters.

If you're buying cooked lobsters, start here. Separate the claws and tail from the body: this can be done simply by twisting them. Now it's time to pick out the tail meat. Try to keep it whole and pull it out in one piece, cutting down the back and discarding the intestinal vein. Put it onto a plate. Crack the claws with a nutcracker and pick the meat out into a bowl. Reserve the body shells. You are now ready to start cooking the different dishes.

To make the lobster bisque, heat the oil and butter in a large saucepan over a high heat and fry the lobster body shells for 5 minutes or until coloured and fragrant. Remove the shells and add the celery, garlic, onions, fennel, chilli and spices, then cook over a low heat for 5 minutes.

Add the tomato purée and cook for 1 minute. Then deglaze the pan with the Pernod, stirring to pick up the flavours in the pan. Add the wine and stock, then return the lobster body shells to the pan. Add the bay leaves, lemon zest and tarragon, and cook over a low heat for 30 minutes.

Pass the liquid through a fine sieve, discarding the other ingredients, then return it to the pan and cook over a high heat to reduce it by about one-quarter; this will take about 5 minutes. Stir in the cream and lemon juice, and season with salt and pepper to taste. Keep aside until ready to serve.

To make the lobster claw toasts, put the claw meat in the bowl of a food processor and add the lemon zest, spring onion, chives and egg. Season with salt and pepper, then blitz. (Alternatively, chop the ingredients finely using a sharp knife, then put in a bowl. Beat the egg and stir it in.) Spread this wet mix on top of the bread slices.

Add the oil to a depth of 1cm in a large frying pan and heat until hot. Fry the toasts, lobster side down first. Turn over after 1 minute and fry for another 1 minute on the other side until golden. Put to one side until ready to serve.

To make the tarragon dip, put the mayonnaise and crème fraîche in a bowl and add the lime zest and juice and the tarragon. Mix well and season to taste with salt and pepper.

To make the summer vegetable and lobster cigars, shred the tail meat lengthways into long strips and place in a bowl. Add the lime zest and juice and the mint, and season with salt and pepper. Put to one side.

Lay out the spring roll pastry sheets, then cut each square in half diagonally to make eight triangles. Put the shredded lobster meat and courgette strips on the wide side of each triangle, then brush the edges of the pastry with the egg and roll up. Fold over the ends to close. The rolls are now ready to fry.

Fill a deep-fryer or a large heavy-based saucepan one-third full with oil and heat it to 175°C (test by frying a small cube of bread; it should brown in 40 seconds). Add the rolls and fry until golden. Serve the lobster cigars alongside the tarragon dip as a starter. Then when you're ready for the bisque, warm it up on the stove and heat the toasts in a preheated oven for a few minutes so they are warm and crispy to serve.

WEST BRITON CRAB CLAWS WITH LEMON AND GARLIC BROTH

Serves 4

A fabulously messy thing to eat, these claws are served on a thick base of newspaper (the *West Briton* is particularly good!) with a hammer, a shellfish pick, a bucket for the shells and a bowl of lemon water for rinsing your hands.

1kg cooked crab claws
200g butter, softened
5 garlic cloves, crushed
a handful of parsley
    leaves, chopped
3 tbsp olive oil
crusty bread, to serve
newspaper (*West Briton*
    ideally!), a hammer,
    or nut crackers, and
    shellfish picks or
    skewers

FOR THE BROTH
200g butter
5 garlic cloves, crushed
1 lemon, cut into 8 wedges
2 bay leaves
200ml white wine
20g tarragon sprigs
10 black peppercorns
10 coriander seeds
2 tbsp sea salt

First, make the broth. Take a large saucepan that will hold the claws, add the butter and melt it over a medium heat. Add the garlic, lemon and bay leaves, and cook until the garlic just starts to colour. Pour in the wine and cook until reduced by half and there is no smell of alcohol. Add the remaining broth ingredients and 300ml water, then bring to the boil. Reduce the heat to a simmer and cook for 5 minutes.

Increase the heat to bring the broth to a gentle boil, then add the crab claws and return to the boil. Reduce the heat and simmer for 5 minutes to heat through.

Transfer the crab claws and broth to a large serving bowl. Put the butter in a separate bowl and add the garlic, parsley and olive oil. Mix together well, then spoon over the hot crab claws and broth to make a buttery sauce.

Cover your table with sheets of the newspaper of your choice and put the bowl of crab claws and broth in the middle. You will also need a small hammer or nut crackers, a bucket for the shells and a bowl of lemon water for rinsing your hands.

To eat, scoop the crab claws out of the broth and crack with the hammer using just enough pressure to crack the shell without shattering it into lots of small pieces. Pull out the meat using the hard cartilage in the centre of the claw to help; if you are lucky it will come out in one piece. Alternatively, extract or pick out the meat using a shellfish pick or skewer. Mop up the buttery cooking broth with plenty of crusty bread.

63   Noon

FRITTO MISTO

There are no rules as to what you fry when making a fritto misto – it's about a collection of flavours and textures. I've added some seafood here, but you can keep it veggie if you prefer. If you do include seafood in your fritto misto, put some aioli (see page 90) out on the table too.

Serves 4

sunflower oil, for
    deep-frying
1 small butternut squash,
    peeled, deseeded and
    finely sliced lengthways
1 fennel bulb, finely
    sliced lengthways
1 red onion, finely
    sliced lengthways
2 red peppers, deseeded
    and finely sliced
    lengthways
500g squid, cleaned, body
    sliced into fine rings and
    tentacles left whole
1 lemon, finely sliced
    into rings
a handful of drained tinned
    chickpeas, rinsed
1 chilli, finely chopped
a handful of mixed
    soft herbs
sea salt and freshly
    ground black pepper
2 lemons, cut into wedges,
    to serve

FOR THE BATTER
125g cornflour
125g plain flour
1 tsp baking powder
a pinch of sea salt
juice of 1 lemon

To make the batter, sift the dry ingredients into a bowl. Slowly add 275ml cold water while whisking to form a lump-free batter. Add the lemon juice and whisk once more. Put to one side while you prep your veg.

Fill a deep-fryer or a heavy-based saucepan one-third full with oil and heat it to 180°C (test by frying a small cube of bread; it should brown in 40 seconds). Dip the squash slices into the batter and then lower each one carefully into the hot oil. Cook for 3 minutes or until they start to caramelise then lift out of the pan using a slotted spoon and drain off the excess oil. Place on a few sheets of kitchen paper and dab dry.

Batter and cook the remaining vegetables, squid, lemon slices, chickpeas and chilli in the same way, although the softer ingredients will take slightly less time: 1–2 minutes.

Batter and fry the herbs separately – they will take less than a minute. Season all the battered ingredients with salt and pepper. Serve as a beautiful stack in the centre of the table, with wedges of lemon.

SCALLOP SALAD WITH HOG'S PUDDING, GINGERED PEAR AND WATERCRESS SALAD

Serves 4

Here is a classy lunch that is surprisingly simple to achieve. The flavours in this salad are quintessentially Cornish with the salty hog's pudding and the delicate umami of the local scallops. The sweet and bitter notes of the gingered pear and watercress bring it all together. It is great with a glass of Camel Valley fizz.

2 pears, peeled, quartered and cored
a squeeze of lemon juice
sunflower oil, for frying
100g hog's pudding, cut into matchsticks
12 Cornish king scallops, corals removed and discarded and white meat halved horizontally
100g watercress, thick stalks discarded

FOR THE DRESSING
10g piece of fresh root ginger, peeled and grated
2 tbsp orange juice
½ tsp Dijon mustard
1 tbsp mild olive oil
sea salt and freshly ground black pepper

First poach the pears. Put the pear quarters in a saucepan and just cover with water. Add the lemon juice, which will help stop the pears discolouring. Bring to the boil over a high heat, then reduce the heat and simmer gently for 10–20 minutes, depending a lot on the ripeness of the fruit, until the pears are tender and a knife can be easily inserted. Remove the pan from the heat, but leave the pears in the water to keep warm while you prepare the other bits.

To make the dressing, put the ginger in a mortar. Add the orange juice and mustard, then grind with a pestle to blend it. Add the oil and season well with salt and pepper, then put to one side.

Heat a drizzle of sunflower oil in a frying pan over a high heat and fry the hog's pudding for 3–4 minutes, stirring frequently, until it crisps up.

In a separate frying pan, heat another drizzle of oil over a high heat. Sear the scallops for 1 minute on the first side without moving them, then turn them over and cook for 30 seconds on the other side.

For individual servings, divide the watercress between four plates and add two of the pear quarters. Sprinkle the hog's pudding pieces over the top, then add six scallop halves to each plate. Finish with a drizzle of the dressing. You can also arrange the salad on one large serving platter and allow everyone to help themselves, depending on the occasion.

SPIDER CRAB LINGUINE

Don't be put off by the name or the freakish look of these wonderful other-worldly creatures of the deep. They are abundant, scuttling around the Cornish shores; yet most catches get exported to the continent. The meat of spider crab is considered a delicacy in Spain. Over here, it's only recently starting to be appreciated. For this reason, spider crab is both a sustainable and great-value local seafood choice. The sweet meat, while awkward to pick from those long spindly legs, is well worth the effort.

Two good-sized hen spider crabs (or one large cock crab) will give you enough crab meat to feed four people this crab linguine.

Serves 4

2 × 1.5kg cooked hen spider crabs (or 1 × 2kg cock crab) – you will need about 75g brown meat and 20g white crab meat per person
400g dried linguine pasta
4 tbsp olive oil
2 garlic cloves, thinly sliced
2 red chillies, deseeded and finely sliced
200ml white wine
100g butter
a bunch of flat-leaf parsley, leaves roughly chopped
a little lemon juice
sea salt and freshly ground black pepper

First prepare the crabs. Put one of the cooked crabs on its back, with its underside facing up, on a chopping board. Twist off the legs and claws, and set aside. Holding on to the shell, firmly press and pull the underside of the crab away from the top shell in one piece. Remove and discard the long white feathery gills (also known as 'dead man's fingers') around the main body as well as the grey-white stomach sac.

Cut the body in half with a knife, and scrape and pick the white meat out of the body and into a bowl. Take your time, as there is a surprising amount of meat hiding in the small cavities. Scoop the brown meat out of the shell – the quantity will depend on the time of the year and the size of the crab – and into a separate bowl.

Crack the claws with a small hammer or nutcrackers and use a skewer or crab/lobster pick to prise out the white meat before placing in the white-meat bowl – you may be able to pull it out in one piece with your fingers, using the shard of hard cartilage in the centre to help. Repeat with the legs, breaking them at the joints and picking out the meat. Follow this method with the rest of the crabs, checking for any stray pieces of shell, then set aside.

Cook the pasta in boiling salted water according to the packet instructions. While it is cooking, put the oil, garlic and chillies in a saucepan over a low heat and cook for 1 minute or until softened. Add the white wine, increase the heat to medium and cook until reduced by half. Add the brown crab meat and the butter, then heat through until the butter has melted.

Drain the pasta, saving a few tablespoons of the cooking water. Add the pasta and the saved cooking water to the pan with the crab, tossing to coat in the sauce.

Take the pan off the heat and fold in the white crab meat and parsley, then finish with a squeeze of lemon juice. Season well with salt and black pepper, and serve.

How to cook over fire

Cooking over a wood fire in the open air is a special part of our work here in Cornwall. It's what we're about and it's at the heart of our outdoor feast nights. I love the challenge and thought that's required for this style of cooking; you can't just turn on the electricity or light the gas. It requires planning and preparation. It slows everything down, in a good way, turning supper into a ritual with warmth and theatre. It's definitely something to be enjoyed with friends and family.

No two fires are the same. There are so many variables to consider when cooking over natural fuel, from differences in equipment and the type of fuel used to the air temperature, and even the speed of the wind. You have to cook with your senses and learn to trust your instincts. It's cooking off-grid, and is an entirely different experience to cooking in a conventional kitchen. But the resulting flavours you get are incomparable – from delicately infused paella to a smokey, chargrilled rib of beef with dark caramelised bark. It's definitely worth the adventure.

71 Noon

Choosing the right equipment

You don't have to spend lots of cash on fancy top-of-the-range kit. A grill rack balanced on a few bricks over a fire can be all you need.

I love the challenge of building an upcycled grill – we've made them from tractor wheels, iron pans, huge colanders and washing-machine drums. Obviously, we're cooking on a much larger scale than you're likely to be at home, but there are still lots of options for you to choose from.

The first thing, whether you go for a fire pit, a large asado-type grill or a charcoal barbecue, is to get to know your kit and how it cooks. Everyone's grill cooks differently, but time and experience will ensure that you learn how to manage and regulate the heat and get the best from your equipment.

Fire pit on the beach

For me, this is the ultimate in wild cooking. All you need is a spade to dig a hole in the ground, a heavy-duty wire grill rack, tongs, a lighter, tea towel and a fishing rod. OK, you don't have to catch your own fish, but it's great if you can.

Before you start, make sure that fires are allowed by the local council, assess the wind direction and set everything up away from any trees or plants that could catch fire. It goes without saying: always choose a non-flammable surface such as sand, stones, earth or gravel when building a fire pit. Gather the largest stones you can find and use them to line the pit, to a depth of about 25cm. The stones will help to retain the heat from the fire.

At ground level, place large stones around the perimeter of the pit for the grill rack to sit on. Now search for kindling, making sure it is dry. Light your fire following the instructions on page 76 (Lighting a Wood Fire), and just before you're ready to cook, put the rack on top and you're good to go. Whole wild seabass is amazing cooked in this way – see the recipe for it on page 80.

Wood-fired asado grill

These are amazing for cooking large cuts of meat, low and slow. If you're starting from scratch, consider a permanent brick or stone grill, which can accommodate a grill rack and a wood cage. They work by burning wood in the cage away from the cooking area. Once the logs are alight and smouldering, you agitate the cage and wood coals fall onto the solid base of the grill. These can then be raked across to underneath your grilling area either directly underneath for direct heat, or just to the side for indirect heat. You'll need a good wood supplier, as you'll be cooking for long periods and they tend to use the most fuel. The flavour from the asado is incredible: it's like a slow, smokey cooker – fantastic for meat that has lots of fat, such as lamb shoulder or pork belly.

Charcoal barbecue

The beauty of charcoal is that it gives you a shorter, more intense cook that is very predictable. Perfect for small items such as sausages, vegetables or sardines. When choosing a barbecue, try to find one with a large surface area and options for different shelf heights. Variable air vents are helpful, too. For an extra hit of smokiness, add green wood or soaked hardwood split logs directly to the hot coals.

Getting organised

Part of the richness of enjoying the grill is in the preparation. I like to get everything ready the day before, or if that's not possible, to at least set it up first thing, and it is essential to never put your grill away without cleaning it properly after using it.

- After grilling, always give the grill rack a good scrub down with a wire brush to remove any fat and sticky bits. We normally dig up the hot coals and tip them over the wire rack after cooking in order to burn off any debris. If you've got any woody herbs, put them on the hot coals and the oils will leach onto the grill. Then, when you come back to the grill to clean it, it smells great and just needs a brush.

- Before you start grilling again, make sure your grill is clean. We rub the cut half of an onion over the grill rack before cooking, which magically cleans it as well as making it non-stick.

- Always cook with the best fresh ingredients your money can buy. The better the quality, the better the end result. If grilling low and slow, you want a cut of meat that suits this method of cooking – get to know your butcher, who will be able to give you invaluable advice. Similarly, a fishmonger will be able to recommend suitable seafood for grilling. For me, lobster, mackerel, crab and whole sea bass are all magic cooked over a wood fire.

- For an extra layer of flavour, a rub or marinade can take it to another level, as well as tenderising the food. Allow enough time for the flavours to infuse – no less than an hour, though overnight is best if there's time. A dry rub will give a great crust to slow-cooked food, whereas a marinade is best for grilling.

Setting up your grill

You don't need to spend a lot on tools. The following are useful, rather than must-haves, but they will make your cooking easier.

- Wood-fire tool box, so that all your barbecue equipment is kept in one place.
- Thermometer probe to check for perfect doneness.
- Heatproof gloves – I use heavy-duty leather welding ones, but then again I'm cooking over industrial-sized grills.
- Long-arm tongs for moving food around and putting on/taking off the grill.
- Goggles – military are my choice, but just sunglasses will help if that's all you have.
- Heavy-duty apron.
- Closed footwear that you're not precious about - you don't want to be wearing flip-flops near hot coals!
- Sharp knives.
- Brushes for basting meat and fish.
- Cast iron pans.

Fuel
My fuel of choice is wood, depending on what I'm cooking. We have created a wood library where we have eight different types of wood seasoned and ready to cook with. Ultimately, you want a little moisture in the wood, around 18–20 per cent, to give smoke and not just white-hot heat.

Fruit woods, such as apple, cherry or pear, lend their own distinctive, fragrant flavour and aroma, but oak and beech are great all-rounders with a good smokiness. Hickory and mesquite add a distinctive smokey flavour, but they are strong, so use sparingly.

If charcoal is your fuel of choice, look for lumpwood, which burns at a high heat for a decent length of time. Or you could combine charcoal with wood – a couple of damp logs on top will get the smoke going. The good thing about charcoal is that it is more predictable than wood, but you don't get quite the same depth of flavour as you do with pure wood.

Lighting a wood fire

To start a wood fire for cooking over you need time, patience and vigilance, and it goes without saying that you must never leave your fire unattended. It's also different from starting a charcoal one in that it needs more time to get established and reach a good heat – at least 1 hour for wood compared with about 30 minutes for charcoal.

To get things started, avoid chemical-based fire lighters and go natural, choosing kindling, dried twigs, crumpled newspaper and dried leaves instead. Put a small pyramid-shaped pile in the centre of your pit, grill or bowl, and light it. When the fire gets going, now's the time to add a few split logs or chunks of dry seasoned firewood in a loose small stack on top of and/or around the edge of the fire. Don't overload the fire with wood; you need ventilation and oxygen to let it 'breathe'. If your fire is struggling to get going or starts to die, give it a poke with a fire poker to agitate the logs. You could also blow on it.

When the wood begins to burn down, add more logs or chunks to maintain the fire and create a decent bed of burning embers. One common mistake many make is to start cooking too quickly. Wait for the flames to die down to glowing embers, unless you like burnt food. Once the fire has got going, I like to place a few logs that have been soaked in water on top to add extra smokiness.

Now's the time to put the rack over the fire. As mentioned earlier, I rub it with the cut side of an onion to stop food from sticking; it is also better than using oil, which can lead to flare-ups.

Hot 'n fast or low 'n slow?

Now the fire is ready, it's time to decide how you want to cook your food. A general guide is that food that takes less than 30 minutes to cook can be grilled directly over the embers, whereas anything that requires more time should be cooked over indirect heat (see overleaf). Over time, and with experience, you'll master how to control and monitor the temperature of your grill using direct or indirect heat, or by combining the two, otherwise known as two-zone cooking.

77   Noon

Direct cooking

This is when you want to cook hot and fast. Food is placed on the grill rack directly over a single layer of glowing embers or hot coals (not flames), which is perfect if you want to seal or sear, say, a steak. Be warned, though, you need to keep an eye on things, as you don't want to incinerate the food. For a more controllable heat, let the coals or wood cool down slightly to a medium heat.

Indirect cooking

Ideal for cooking large roasts low and slow, this method gives a lovely smokiness. The heat source and the food are kept separate to prevent the food cooking too quickly – the coals are raked so that they are positioned below but just to the side of your cooking space. If you need to keep the heat going for a long time, just throw a split log or two, or some wood chunks or charcoal, on the fuel side, away from the cooking food.

Two-zone cooking

This is my go-to method of choice. The two zones (direct and indirect) will give you a range of temperatures and is perfect if you're cooking more than one dish or if, for example, you have a large joint of meat that requires initial searing on the direct hot part of the grill and then moving to the indirect part for low-and-slow cooking.

If cooking low and slow, you need to set up a 'coal-making station' to one side of the grill to sustain the heat of the grill for long periods. This will enable you to burn wood or charcoal away from the food and rake the glowing embers underneath the grilling food when needed.

To set this up, once your grill is ready to cook over, brush the hot embers to one side (this is your coal-making station). You'll need to add extra fuel to the piled-up embers if they start to die down and to keep the fire/heat going. If the heat dies down too much on the indirect side, just rake some of the glowing embers back over.

TIPS FOR COOKING OVER FIRE

- Get ahead – light your wood fire at least 1 hour in advance of cooking and a charcoal one about 30 minutes before.

- Avoid putting your food on the grill too early; wait for the flames to die down to glowing embers.

- Be conservative when oiling food, as too much can drip through the grate and lead to flare-ups.

- Make a herb whip using long sprigs of woody herbs, such as rosemary, bay and thyme, tied together at the top. We often use big bunches of herbs for basting meat and fish when cooking.

- Keep a bowl of brine made from water, lemon juice and salt to one side when cooking – you can splash it onto the embers to calm them down and prevent flare-ups, and it's also good for seasoning food.

- Cooking over fire is a bit of an unknown quantity; it's tricky to give exact cooking times when there are so many variables at play, but a thermometer can help you check for doneness.

- You've lovingly prepared and cooked your meat; now don't stint on the resting time. Depending on the cut and size of the joint, 20–30 minutes should be enough to allow the meat to settle and to make sure it's juicy and tender.

- Have fun, enjoy the experience – pull up a deck chair and get ready for a relaxed day of cooking by the grill.

FIRE-PIT WILD SEA BASS WITH VERDE SAUCE

A real crowd pleaser, this chargrilled whole fish is just beautiful in its simplicity. Stuffed with soft herbs and slices of lemon and garlic, the fish is cooked until the skin turns crisp, with striking grill lines. It comes with a slightly sharp herby sauce, which adds a burst of greenness as well as lots of flavour.

Serves 4–6

1 × 2kg wild sea bass, gutted and scaled
olive oil, for coating
2 handfuls of flat-leaf parsley leaves
leaves from a handful of lemon thyme sprigs
1 large lemon, sliced
1 large garlic clove, thinly sliced
5 bay leaves
½ onion
extra-virgin olive oil, for drizzling
lemon wedges and crusty bread, to serve

FOR THE VERDE SAUCE
7 anchovy fillets in vinegar, or 4 if using salted
10g wild garlic leaves or 1 garlic clove, peeled
2 tbsp capers
20g basil leaves
15g flat-leaf parsley leaves
1 heaped tbsp lemon thyme leaves
juice of ½ lemon
125ml extra-virgin olive oil
sea salt and freshly ground black pepper

To make the verde sauce, rinse the anchovies if using salted, then put them and the remaining ingredients, apart from the olive oil, into a mini food processor and blitz until finely chopped. Gradually pour in the olive oil and blend to a fairly smooth sauce, then season with salt and pepper. (Alternatively, if you prefer a chunkier sauce, finely chop the anchovies, garlic, capers and herbs, or use a pestle and mortar, then add the lemon juice. Gradually stir in the oil.) Spoon the sauce into a bowl and set aside.

Light the fire pit (or you could use a wood-fired grill or a barbecue) about 30 minutes before cooking, following the instructions on page 76. You want a medium-high heat on one half of the fire-pit grill (check out the method for two-zone cooking on page 78). The rack should be about 20cm above the heat source.

Rinse the sea bass in cold running water, then pat dry inside and out with kitchen paper. You could cut a slash behind the head to enable heat to reach the collar, but I don't tend to slash the sides – the skill is in creating bass crackling.

Rub the fish all over with a good coating of olive oil. Stuff the parsley, thyme, lemon slices and garlic into the fish cavity, then top with the bay leaves. Season with salt and pepper.

Rub the grill rack with the cut side of the onion to stop the fish sticking to it, then put the sea bass directly on the hot side of the fire-pit grill. Grill the sea bass for 4 minutes on each side, carefully turning/rolling it over using two fish slices. Move the fish over to the cooler side of the grill and cook for 3 minutes on each side or until the skin is crisp and the flesh starts to flake away from the bone, especially around the base of the head.

Serve the sea bass with a splash of olive oil and the lemon wedges, verde sauce and chunky slices of crusty bread.

Summer Sardines

These grilled sardines are served with saffron potatoes, vine tomatoes and samphire with an oregano dressing – the makings of a perfect summer's afternoon. The oregano dressing is best made using a mortar and pestle to break down the plant matter and really bring out the herbal flavour.

Serves 8

400g samphire
8 × 100g stems of cherry
    tomatoes on the vine
24 sardines about 70–90g
    each, gutted, scaled
    and trimmed
olive oil, for drizzling

FOR THE SAFFRON
POTATOES

8 large waxy potatoes,
    peeled and halved
250g butter
200ml chicken stock
4 garlic cloves, crushed
    lightly with the side
    of a knife
juice of 1 lemon
a pinch of saffron threads
sea salt and freshly ground
    black pepper

FOR THE OREGANO
DRESSING

2 garlic cloves, peeled
a large handful of
    oregano leaves
4 tsp sea salt
juice of 2 lemons
300ml extra-virgin olive oil

First make the saffron potatoes. Trim off the curves of each potato to make them flat on the top and bottom. Heat the butter in a large saucepan over a medium heat. When the butter is foaming, add the potatoes and fry until deep golden brown on one side, about 5 minutes – do not move the potatoes as they cook.

Turn the potatoes over and cook for a further 5 minutes, until golden brown on both sides. Carefully pour in the stock, watching out for any splutter from when the the stock meets the hot fat, then add the garlic cloves, lemon juice and saffron. Season with a little salt and pepper. Cover the pan with a lid and when the stock is simmering, reduce the heat. Simmer the potatoes for 10–12 minutes or until tender, then remove them from the pan using a slotted spoon and keep warm.

Meanwhile, prepare and heat up your barbecue, if using, or preheat the grill to high. Preheat the oven to 200°C (180°C fan oven) gas mark 6.

To make the oregano dressing, crush the garlic with the oregano and sea salt to a paste using a mortar and pestle, then stir in the lemon juice and slowly add the oil.

Put the samphire and tomatoes in a baking dish, dress with a little olive oil and salt and roast in the oven for 8 minutes. Take out and dress with the oregano dressing. Season the sardines with salt and pepper and cook them on the barbecue grill rack or under the hot grill, close to the heat, for 1–2 minutes on each side or until nicely charred. Serve the sardines on top of the tomatoes and samphire to allow the natural oils to infuse, with the warm saffron potatoes alongside.

86   Noon

87 Noon

CRAB RAREBIT

I think this is probably my favourite thing on toast. It's simple, but it punches some amazing Cornish flavours with the fresh crab and local cheese.

25g butter
25g plain flour
200ml whole milk
50g Cheddar cheese, grated
1 tsp English mustard
1 tsp Worcestershire sauce
200g cooked white crab meat, flaked
a small handful of chives, snipped
4 slices of your favourite bread (sourdough is what I'd choose for this)
50g cooked brown crab meat, flaked
sea salt and freshly ground black pepper

Preheat the grill to high. Melt the butter in a heavy-based pan over a low heat. Add the flour and cook for 2 minutes, stirring all the time. Add the milk, stirring to blend it smoothly. Cook for 3–4 minutes to cook out the taste of the flour and thicken the sauce.

Take the pan off the heat and add the grated cheese, mustard and Worcestershire sauce, then mix thoroughly. Add the white crab meat and chives, and stir in.

Lightly grill one side of your bread slices. Take out of the grill and lightly spread the brown crab meat over the untoasted side of the bread. Top evenly with the white crab mix. Grill for 4 minutes until golden and crispy on top, and serve.

CRISPY SALT COD AND POTATO BALLS

When you bite into these, it's a delight to discover the juicy, salty treasure in the middle. Surrounded by a good layer of potato and breadcrumbs, the salt cod is not overpowering at all. Just don't try to use mashed potato instead of baked; you'll end up with cracked potato balls. Which isn't a good look...

Serves 4

700g large baking
    potatoes, unpeeled
    and scrubbed
25g butter
6 spring onions,
    finely chopped
a bunch of dill fronds,
    chopped
200g salt cod, cut into
    16 chunks, 2cm each
100g plain flour
3 eggs, beaten
200g panko breadcrumbs
sunflower oil, for
    deep-frying

FOR THE AIOLI
1 egg yolk
juice of 1 lemon
70ml extra-virgin olive oil
50ml sunflower oil
2 garlic cloves
sea salt and freshly ground
    black pepper

Preheat the oven to 210°C (190°C fan oven) gas mark 6½ and bake the potatoes whole for 1½ hours or until soft when squeezed. Leave until cool enough to handle, then cut in half and scoop the fluffy dry potato from the skins into a bowl, and mash with the butter, spring onions and dill.

To make the aioli, put the egg yolk and half the lemon juice into a blender and blitz. Add each oil really slowly, trickling it in in a very thin stream, until it's all been added. Once all the oil has been added, stop blending. Alternatively, if you don't have a blender, you can do this in a mixing bowl using a whisk.

Pulverise the garlic with ½ teaspoon salt using a mortar and pestle (or bash it with the end of a rolling pin in a small bowl) until puréed to a paste, then mix it into the mayonnaise. Stir in more of the lemon juice to taste and season with salt and pepper. Put to one side.

Put the salt cod in a bowl and pour over boiling water to cover. Leave for 3 minutes to soften in the water.

Divide the potato into 16 even portions and wrap it around the cod. Cover with cling film and put in the fridge for 30 minutes.

Put the flour in a shallow bowl and season with salt and pepper. Put the eggs in another shallow bowl and the panko breadcrumbs in a third. Coat the balls in the flour, then in the egg, then the breadcrumbs, then in the egg again, and finally in the breadcrumbs once more.

Fill a deep-fryer or a large heavy-based saucepan one-third full with sunflower oil and heat it to 180°C (test by frying a small cube of bread; it should brown in 40 seconds). Fry the balls for 2½ minutes or until golden and crispy. Serve with the aioli for dipping.

NEWLYN OCTOPUS

Cornish octopus is one of those underrated local catches that get snapped up by the export market. It's affordable, healthy and delicious – I'm always surprised that we don't use it more often locally. Here is a really simple and fresh way to serve it.

Serves 4

700g cleaned octopus
(3–4 in total)
2 tbsp olive oil
zest of 1 lemon and 1 tbsp
lemon juice
1 tbsp sherry vinegar
sea salt and freshly ground
black pepper

**FOR THE ROASTED
TOMATOES**
500g cherry tomatoes
on the vine
1 garlic bulb, cloves peeled
and halved
1 lemon, cut into wedges
2 tbsp olive oil, plus extra
for drizzling
a good handful of basil
leaves, ripped

Put the octopus in a large saucepan of salted water over a high heat and bring to the boil, then reduce the heat and simmer for 45–50 minutes until tender right through when tested with a knife. Remove the pan from the heat and leave the octopus to cool in the water in the pan for another 15 minutes.

Preheat the oven to 240°C (220°C fan oven) gas mark 9. To make the roasted tomatoes, take the tomatoes off the vine and put them on a baking tray. Add the garlic and lemon wedges. Drizzle everything with a good glug of olive oil and toss to coat well. Roast for 15 minutes or until the tomatoes are beginning to collapse and the garlic is softened.

Meanwhile, take the tentacles off the octopus, and slice them smaller if they are really big. Slice the bodies into rings. Put them all in a bowl and add the olive oil, lemon zest and juice, sherry vinegar and 1 teaspoon salt, then toss to coat well.

Heat a griddle pan until burning hot. Spread the octopus out on the griddle and sear for 5 minutes, turning regularly.

Transfer the tomatoes, garlic and lemons to a serving platter using a slotted spoon. Add the 2 tablespoons olive oil to the juices in the baking tray and mix together to make a dressing. Season to taste with salt and pepper. Drizzle the juices over the platter and sprinkle over the ripped basil leaves. Top with the charred octopus and serve.

Red-Hot
Mullet
with
Sticky Rice
Balls and
Cucumber
Salad

Red-Hot Mullet with Sticky Rice Balls and Cucumber Salad

Small and delicate red mullet lend themselves so well to a tempura coating. The sparkling water in the batter mix gives the goujons a super-light and crispy finish. Dip the goujons and sticky rice balls into the hot coconut masala and enjoy the refreshing cucumber salad on the side.

Serves 8

8 red mullet fillets (about 80–100g each) boned and skinned
400g self-raising flour
4 tbsp cornflour
8 tsp ground turmeric
1 tsp paprika
zest and juice of 2 lemons
500ml sparkling water
200g plain flour
sunflower oil, for deep-frying
fine sea salt

Wash the rice for the sticky rice balls in cold water until the water runs clear of rice starch, then leave the rice to soak in 625ml clean water for 30 minutes to allow it to expand. Put the rice and the soaking water in a large saucepan with a lid. Bring the rice to the boil, then reduce the heat and simmer gently, covered, for 12 minutes. The water should have soaked into the cooked rice. Leave the rice to stand for a further 10 minutes. Never remove the lid during this process.

Once cooked, tip the rice onto a baking tray and spread it out to cool.

Slice each of the red mullet fillets lengthways into three pieces. Put the self-raising flour, cornflour, 2 teaspoons salt and the spices in a bowl and add the lemon zest, then mix together. Mix the lemon juice with the sparkling water and gently whisk into the dry ingredients. Leave this batter to rest for 30 minutes.

To make the coconut masala, put the cumin seeds in a small dry saucepan and add the coriander, fenugreek and mustard seeds. Toast them over a medium-high heat for 2 minutes or until fragrant and crackling. Grind together using a mortar and pestle, then stir in the turmeric and curry powder.

FOR THE STICKY RICE BALLS

500g sushi rice
60ml white wine vinegar
60g caster sugar
20g sea salt
6 tbsp black and white
    sesame seeds
sesame oil, for drizzling

FOR THE HOT COCONUT MASALA

2 tbsp cumin seeds
2 tbsp coriander seeds
2 tsp fenugreek seeds
    (or leaves)
2 tsp mustard seeds
½ tsp ground turmeric
1 tbsp curry powder
3 onions, chopped
100g piece of fresh root
    ginger, peeled
    and roughly chopped
3 red chillies, deseeded
    and chopped
40g coriander leaves, plus
    1 tbsp chopped
    coriander leaves
2 tbsp vegetable oil
4 tbsp desiccated coconut
2 tbsp tomato purée
400g tin chopped
    tomatoes
2 tbsp caster sugar
1½ tbsp fine sea salt
juice of 2 lemons
2 tsp garam masala
400ml coconut milk

FOR THE CUCUMBER SALAD

30g coriander leaves,
    finely chopped
20g mint leaves,
    finely chopped
juice of 4 limes
juice of 2 lemons
2 tsp caster sugar
1 tsp fine sea salt
4 cucumbers, peeled
8 spring onions, finely
    sliced on the diagonal

Put the onions in a blender and add the ginger, chillies, the 40g coriander leaves, vegetable oil and the desiccated coconut. Blitz together to make a paste.

Cook the curry paste in a dry frying pan over a medium-high heat for 2 minutes. Add the spice mix and cook for another minute. Add the tomato purée, tomatoes, 100ml water and the sugar and salt, and cook for a further 20 minutes over a low heat.

Meanwhile, to make the cucumber salad, put the herbs in a large bowl and add the citrus juices, sugar and salt. Mix well. Using a swivel vegetable peeler, cut the cucumbers into ribbons, stopping when you reach the seeds and discarding them. Add to the bowl, followed by the spring onions, and toss in the dressing.

Put the wine vinegar for the sticky rice in a bowl and add the sugar and salt. Mix well together, stirring constantly, until the sugar and salt have dissolved. Pour this seasoning mix over the cool rice and mix very well using a wooden spoon.

Put the sesame seeds in a shallow bowl. With wet hands, roll the rice into 24 golf-ball-sized balls and roll them in the sesame seeds until completely covered. Line a flat roasting tin with baking parchment and lay out the rice balls, then drizzle them with sesame oil. Preheat the oven to 210°C (190°C fan oven) gas mark 6½. Roast the rice balls for 15 minutes or until the sesame seeds have given them a crispy and golden toasted crust.

Blitz the coconut masala in a blender until smooth, then return it to the pan and stir in the lemon juice, garam masala, coconut milk and the 1 tablespoon chopped coriander. Heat through over a low heat.

To prepare the fish, sift the plain flour and 1 teaspoon salt into a bowl. Whisk the rested batter again before using. Dip the fish goujons into the flour mix then the batter mix, making sure they are evenly coated all over.

Fill a deep-fryer or a large heavy-based saucepan one-third full with sunflower oil and heat it to 180°C (test by frying a small cube of bread; it should brown in 40 seconds). Deep-fry the goujons for 2 minutes or until crisp. Sprinkle with salt to serve. Give everyone individual ramekins of the coconut masala and then put big dishes in the middle of the table with the sticky rice balls, a stack of goujons and the cucumber salad, and let everyone help themselves.

CEVICHE AT SEA

If you're heading out fishing, take a Tupperware tub of tiger's milk with you, which you will be making using the chilli and limes, and enjoy a memorable ceviche lunch on the boat with the lovely fresh fish that you catch. Alternatively, stay at home in the dry and enjoy with sashimi-grade fish from your local market.

You can use any very fresh, firm-textured white fish, or even scallops, for ceviche. Black bream is a particular favourite of mine.

For maximum flavour, try to get a fruity red chilli, such as Habanero.

Serves 4

4 very fresh firm white fish fillets (about 100g each), skinned
1 small red onion, very finely sliced into rings
10g coriander, leaves roughly chopped and stalks finely chopped, plus a few extra leaves for sprinkling
juice of 8 limes
1 hot red chilli, such as Habanero, deseeded and finely diced
½ tsp granulated sugar
sea salt

Cut a V into the centre of the fish to remove the bloodline and all the pin bones. Take off any little bits of fat, so that you are left with clean white fillets. You don't want any of the red flesh, just the delicate white meat. If you are buying from a fishmonger, they should be able to do this for you.

Slice the fillets thinly, going with the grain of the fish – so you will be cutting down at a slight angle. Try to keep each slice the same thickness, so that they marinate evenly.

Put the red onion in a shallow dish and add the coriander and 1 teaspoon sea salt, then add most of the lime juice with the chilli and a little of the sugar. Adjust the flavour by adding more lime juice, sugar and salt to get a balance of flavours: sharpness from the limes, a bit of saltiness and a little sweetness. Making this mixture – known as tiger's milk – can be a balancing act, depending on the size of the fish, strength of the chillies or tartness of the limes, and so on. Mix it all together and check the flavour.

Spread the fish over a plate and pour the tiger's milk over the fish. Leave to marinate for 5–10 minutes until it starts to whiten. Sprinkle with coriander leaves and serve.

Fried
Buttermilk
Chicken
with
Watermelon
Salsa

Fried Buttermilk Chicken with Watermelon Salsa

Crispy buttermilk chicken with watermelon salsa, charred romaine lettuce, sweet potato fries and lime mayo. This can be enjoyed as a salad, as I've done here, or in a bun for a hand-held lunch.

Soaking chicken in buttermilk tenderises the meat so that it remains soft and juicy after frying. It's well worth the wait. You can make the salsa and lime mayo the day before and soak the chicken overnight if you're short of time on the day. The rest of the ingredients take just minutes to cook.

Serves 8

8 skinless, boneless
   chicken thighs
500ml buttermilk
400g plain flour
3 tbsp smoked paprika
3 tbsp ground cumin
2 tbsp mustard powder
2 tbsp dried oregano
1 tbsp garlic powder
2 tbsp fine sea salt
1 tbsp freshly ground
   black pepper
sunflower oil, for
   deep-frying

**FOR THE WATERMELON
SALSA**

100g peeled and deseeded
   watermelon, blended
   until smooth
1 red chilli, deseeded and
   finely sliced
zest and juice of 1 lime
1 tbsp cider vinegar
2 tbsp caster sugar
1 tbsp honey
1 tsp fine sea salt
100g peeled and deseeded
   watermelon, cut into
   cubes

**FOR THE LIME
MAYONNAISE**

1 tbsp finely chopped
   coriander leaves
a small pinch of fine sea salt
250g good-quality
   mayonnaise
juice of 2 limes

**FOR THE SWEET
POTATO FRIES**

1.2kg sweet potatoes,
   unpeeled, cut into
   thin chips
sunflower oil, for frying
flaked sea salt

**FOR THE CHARRED
ROMAINE LETTUCE**

1 romaine lettuce, cut
   into quarters through
   the core
2 tbsp olive oil
1 tsp fine sea salt

Put a chicken thigh between two sheets of greaseproof paper and bash it with a rolling pin to flatten. Repeat with the other chicken thighs to make them a similar thickness. Put the chicken thighs in a dish and pour over the buttermilk, then leave them to soak for at least 1 hour. If you are a day ahead, overnight is ideal.

To prepare the watermelon salsa, put all ingredients, except for the watermelon cubes, in a pan and cook over a high heat until reduced by about a third, so that the mixture is nice and sticky. Leave to cool.

To make the lime mayonnaise, grind together the coriander and salt using a mortar and pestle to release the flavour. Put the mayonnaise in a bowl and add the coriander mixture and the lime juice. Mix together until well combined. Leave in the fridge until ready to use.

Put the sweet potatoes in a pan of cold water, bring to the boil and cook for 4 minutes. Drain in a colander, then pat dry with kitchen paper and put to one side, ready for frying.

Coat the lettuce quarters in the oil and salt, and cook in a griddle pan over a high heat for 1–2 minutes on all sides until nicely charred. Put to one side.

Lift the chicken out of the buttermilk and wipe off any excess liquid using kitchen paper. Reserve the buttermilk. Put the flour in a bowl and add the spices, mustard powder, oregano, garlic powder, salt and pepper. Use this spiced flour mix to coat the chicken, then dip the chicken back into the buttermilk, and coat with the spiced flour once again.

Preheat the oven to 110°C (90°C fan oven) gas mark ¼ and put a baking tray inside to warm up.

Fill a deep-fryer or a large heavy-based saucepan one-third full with sunflower oil and heat it to 175°C (test by frying a small cube of bread; it should brown in 40 seconds). Fry the chicken for 3 minutes or until cooked through and crispy. Keep warm on the baking tray in the oven.

Fry the sweet potato fries in the oil for 4 minutes until crisp. Season with the flaked salt. Stir the watermelon cubes into the salsa and serve the chicken and fries on the charred romaine with ramekins of watermelon salsa and lime mayo to dip.

CHARRED CHICKEN AND SQUASH SALAD

Bright and colourful, with a creamy goat's cheese dressing and chicken-skin crisps, this is a salad that the whole family will enjoy. The chicken skewers can be cooked indoors on a hot griddle pan or outdoors on the barbecue, depending on the weather.

Serves 4

200g cooked beetroot
juice of 1 orange
2 tbsp cumin seeds
½ tsp black peppercorns
1 tbsp nigella (black onion) seeds
4 chicken breasts, skinned and skins reserved, flesh sliced into strips
sea salt and freshly ground black pepper

FOR THE SQUASH SALAD
1kg butternut squash, peeled, deseeded and cut into 2.5cm chunks
3 tbsp olive oil
leaves from a handful of thyme sprigs
50g pumpkin seeds
4 handfuls of rocket leaves
a bunch of mint, leaves shredded
flaked sea salt

FOR THE CHEESE DRESSING
50g goat's cheese, rind removed
4 tbsp natural yogurt
2 tbsp orange juice

Blitz the beetroot with the orange juice in a food processor, then transfer it to a bowl. Using a mortar and pestle, grind together the cumin seeds, peppercorns and ½ teaspoon salt, then stir this into the beetroot. Add the nigella seeds and the chicken breast strips, then leave to marinate for 2 hours, or overnight if possible.

To make the chicken-skin crisps, preheat the oven to 200°C (180°C fan oven) gas mark 6 and line a baking tray with baking parchment. Cut each of the reserved chicken skins into thirds. Put on the prepared baking tray and season well with salt and pepper. Put another piece of baking parchment over the top and weight it down with another baking tray to stop the skins from curling up while cooking. Cook for 1 hour or until golden and crispy. Put to one side to cool.

To make the squash salad, increase the oven temperature to 220°C (200°C fan oven) gas mark 7. Put the squash into a large baking tray and drizzle over the oil. Season with a good pinch of sea salt flakes and scatter over the thyme leaves. Roast for 40 minutes or until tender and golden brown. Meanwhile, toast the pumpkin seeds in a dry saucepan over a medium-high heat for 3 minutes or until lightly browned, shaking the pan regularly.

To prepare the dressing, put the goat's cheese in a bowl and mash it to a paste, then stir in the yogurt and orange juice. Season with a pinch of salt.

Preheat a griddle pan, or prepare and heat up the barbecue. Spear the chicken strips onto skewers and cook in the griddle pan or on the grill rack of the barbecue for 2 minutes on each side until blackened on the outside.

Toss the warm squash with the rocket leaves. Put the chicken skewers on top. Drizzle with the cheese dressing and sprinkle over the shredded mint and toasted pumpkin seeds. Serve with a bowl of the chicken-skin crisps in the middle to share.

THE CORNISH PASTY

Pasties, like most great inventions in life, were born out of necessity. They filled the need of the Cornish tin miners to have a balanced, sustaining lunch that was robust enough to carry down the underground shafts and insulated enough to stay warm until lunch. The pasties had a thick, crimped edge that wasn't eaten so that they could been held with dirty hands. They were a complete packed lunch in an edible casing. As tin mining in Cornwall began to decline and eventually die out, the Cornish miners migrated further afield to new lands, taking with them their treasured pasty recipes. Pasties, in various forms and adaptations, now exist in mining areas all around the world. From the *paste* in Mexico to beef empanadas in Chile.

Today, the Cornish pasty has Protected Geographical Indication status, so to call a pasty 'Cornish' it has to be made in Cornwall, the Cornish way.

The pasties we serve at the Hidden Hut are locally renowned. People travel far and wide for them. They are authentic perfection and I'm afraid I can't take any of the credit. They are made for us by a small father-and-son pasty bakery in Camborne, called Denzil Trevithick's. This is their family recipe, written word for word, which I am very honoured to share with you in this book.

Makes 4

500g plain flour, plus extra for dusting
1½ tsp sea salt
125g lard, cut into 2cm cubes
75g pastry margarine or vegetable fat, cut into 2cm cubes
75g cold Cornish butter, cut into 2cm cubes

Put the flour and salt into a mixing bowl and mix together. Add the lard and margarine, then rub in using your fingertips until the mixture resembles fine breadcrumbs.

Rub in the butter cubes loosely, working as quickly as possible to prevent the butter becoming too soft. The mixture will be like coarse breadcrumbs with small chunks of butter visible.

Add 75ml very cold water and bring the mixture together using a knife – stirring until the dough binds together. Add more cold water, a teaspoonful at a time, if the mixture is too dry.

200g floury/baking potato
(such as King Edward),
peeled and diced
150g swede, peeled
and diced
150g onions, roughly
chopped
350g beef skirt, diced
1 egg, beaten, to glaze
sea salt and freshly ground
black pepper

Wrap in cling film and leave to rest in the fridge for at least 30 minutes. This is an important stage, as it is almost impossible to roll and shape the pastry when freshly made.

(Alternatively, the dough can be made in a food processor by mixing the flour, salt, lard, and margarine in the bowl of the processor on a pulse setting. Add the butter cubes and distribute through the mixture so that you can still see a few small chunks of butter. When the mixture resembles coarse breadcrumbs, add 75ml water, slowly, through the funnel until the dough comes together in a ball. Wrap and chill as above.)

While the pastry is resting, mix together the vegetables for the filling, then divide them into four portions. Divide the meat into four portions, keeping it separate from the vegetables.

Preheat the oven to 210°C (190°C fan oven) gas mark 6½. Line two large baking sheets with baking parchment. Remove the pastry from the fridge, put onto a floured work surface and roll into a rectangle roughly 30 × 15cm. Fold one-third of the pastry over onto the middle third, then fold the other third on top of these two layers.

Cut into four equal pieces and pat each portion into a round. On a floured work surface, roll out into circles 20cm in diameter – a side plate is an ideal size to use as a guide.

Put a portion of vegetables into the middle of each pastry circle leaving a 2cm clear edge all the way around.

Put the meat on top of the vegetables, and season generously with salt and pepper.

Dip three fingers into a bowl of water and rub all the way around the pastry edges. Fold the pastry over the filling to make a half-moon shape, then bring the dampened edges together and crimp (see How to Crimp overleaf).

Glaze with the beaten egg. Make a steam hole in the centre of each pasty with a sharp knife. Put the pasties on the prepared baking sheets and bake for 30 minutes (see also Top Tips overleaf), swapping the baking sheets around halfway through. Reduce the heat to 200°C (180°C fan oven) gas mark 6 and bake for a further 30 minutes, until golden, swapping the baking sheets around halfway through. Leave the pasties to rest for 5–10 minutes before eating.

108   Noon

How to crimp

Crimping is one of the secrets of a true Cornish pasty. A proper hand crimp is usually a sign of a good handmade pasty. A traditional pasty should be crimped on the side, not across the top; however, it will taste just as good either way! Here's how to crimp a Trevithick's pasty:

- Bring the pastry edges to meet and lightly squeeze the half-circle edges together.

- Push down on the edge of the pasty and, using your index finger and thumb, twist the edge of the pastry over to form a crimp.

- When you've crimped along the edge, tuck the end corners underneath.

Top tips for a perfect pasty

- Beef skirt is the cut traditionally used for Cornish pasties. This is the underside of the belly of the animal. It has no gristle and little fat, it cooks in the same amount of time as the raw vegetables and its juice produces wonderful gravy. A favourite of Trevithick's is to rub cracked black pepper into the skirt before dicing it and putting it onto the vegetables.

- Use a floury or good baking potato, such as King Edward, and ensure that all your veg is freshly prepared.

- Keep your pastry cold!

- Don't make the pastry too wet around edges prior to crimping.

- After the first 15 minutes of cooking, if the crimp has caught, reduce the oven temperature by 10°C.

SEARED SIRLOIN WITH RADISH SALAD

Serves 4

If you're like me and a fiend for salty-bitter flavours, this is the salad for you.

600g sirloin steak, in
    a single piece
olive oil, for rubbing
sea salt

FOR THE RADISH SALAD
1 small mooli (daikon)
    radish, peeled
12 pink radishes, sliced
½ red onion, finely
    sliced into rings
50g samphire
juice of 2 limes
a grating of fresh
    horseradish

FOR THE CAPER DRESSING
4 tbsp drained capers
1 anchovy fillet
extra-virgin olive oil
a squeeze of lemon juice

Preheat the oven to 200°C (180°C fan oven) gas mark 6. Rub the steak with the olive oil and season well with salt. Heat an ovenproof frying pan or griddle pan over a really high heat and add the steak. Cook for 6–8 minutes, turning, until charred all over. Put the pan in the oven and cook for 10 minutes. The steak should still be fairly soft when squeezed and pink in the middle when cut.

Meanwhile, to make the salad, use a swivel vegetable peeler to cut the mooli into ribbons, pressing quite hard so that they are as thick as you can get them.

Put the mooli ribbons in a large bowl and add the pink radishes, onion rings, samphire and lime juice, and toss to coat. Turn out into a serving dish and sprinkle the grated horseradish over the top.

To make the dressing, put the capers and anchovy fillet in a mortar and add the olive oil and lemon juice, then pound to a chunky paste using a pestle.

Remove the beef from the oven and put it on a board. Leave it to rest for 10 minutes, then slice thinly. Spread the caper dressing across the beef and serve with the radish salad.

113 Noon

12-Hour
Lamb and
Smokey
Aubergine

12-Hour Lamb and Smokey Aubergine

The lamb cooks low and slow overnight for about 12 hours, so you can prepare it the night before and enjoy juicy, tender shredded lamb for lunch the next day.

Intensely flavoured and refreshing, this salad is ideal for a long midsummer lunch when aubergines are at their best. If you can't get a local ewe's cheese, feta is a good alternative.

Serves 8

1 × 2.5kg shoulder of lamb
10 garlic cloves, peeled and left whole
2 tsp ground cumin
¼ tsp ground cinnamon
1 tbsp nigella (black onion) seeds
2 star anise
4 cloves
3 red onions, unpeeled and halved
1 tbsp olive oil
150g pomegranate seeds
sea salt and freshly ground black pepper

Preheat the oven to 110°C (90°C fan oven) gas mark ¼. Place the lamb on a large chopping board. Pierce slits in the lamb with the tip of a sharp knife and insert a garlic clove into each one. Sprinkle a good amount of salt and pepper over the top. Sprinkle over the cumin, cinnamon and nigella seeds and rub well into the skin.

Put the onion halves in a deep roasting tin, along with the star anise and cloves. Carefully lay the lamb on top – this prevents the underneath crisping up too much. Drizzle over the oil. Cover the whole tin tightly with foil and roast in the oven for roughly 12 hours or until meltingly tender. Remove from the oven and set aside, covered in foil.

4 large aubergines,
    left whole
juice of 1 lemon
1 tbsp white wine vinegar
3 tbsp extra-virgin olive oil
1 red onion, finely diced
2 red chillies, deseeded and
    finely diced
a bunch of mint, leaves
    finely shredded
1 heaped tsp fine sea salt
a sprinkle of poppy seeds

**FOR THE YOGURT
DRESSING**
400g natural yogurt
1 cucumber, coarsely
    grated or finely chopped
2 tbsp lemon juice
2 handfuls of mint
    leaves, chopped

**FOR THE EWE'S CHEESE
SALAD**
60g pumpkin seeds
160g bulgar wheat
4 tbsp lemon juice
4 tbsp extra-virgin olive oil
80g mint leaves,
    roughly chopped
120g parsley leaves,
    roughly chopped
1 small red onion,
    finely sliced
1.2kg watermelon flesh,
    chopped into 2.5cm
    cubes
350g ewe's cheese or feta
sumac, for sprinkling

Preheat the oven to 240°C (220°C fan oven) gas mark 9. To make the marinated aubergine, heat a large heavy-based frying pan over a high heat. Add the aubergines and cook them, turning occasionally, until softening all over. This gives them their smokey flavour. Transfer them to a baking tray and cook them in the oven for 45 minutes. After 35 minutes of cooking, put the cooked lamb back into the oven with the aubergines, uncovered, to crisp up for the last 10 minutes.

In the meantime, make the yogurt dressing. Put the yogurt in a bowl and stir in the cucumber. Add the lemon juice, mint and a pinch of salt and pepper. Tip into a serving bowl and put to one side.

To make the ewe's cheese salad, toast the pumpkin seeds in a dry saucepan over a medium-high heat for 3 minutes or until lightly browned, shaking the pan regularly. Put to one side.

Place the bulgar wheat in a small saucepan and just cover with water. Put a lid on and cook over a low heat for 8–10 minutes until the water is absorbed and the grains are tender. Leave to cool completely.

Combine the lemon juice and oil in a small bowl and season well with salt and pepper.

In a large mixing bowl, combine the mint, parsley, onion and watermelon. Tip in the lemon juice dressing and toss everything to coat. Transfer the salad to a large serving plate. Crumble the ewe's cheese over the top of the salad, then sprinkle over the toasted pumpkin seeds. Finish with a sprinkle of sumac.

Once the aubergines are ready, let them cool for a few minutes, then peel them, keeping them whole and retaining the stalks at the top to hold them together. Lay them out on a serving plate. The flesh will be falling apart, so open them out a little so that they lie flat. Put the lemon juice, vinegar, oil, onion, chillies and mint in a bowl and season with the salt. Spoon this marinade over the split aubergines and sprinkle with the poppy seeds.

Remove the lamb from the roasting tin and shred it from the bone onto a serving dish. Put the pomegranate seeds into a small bowl with a spoon for sprinkling over the lamb. Lay all the components out on the table and let people help themselves.

LAMB CUTLETS WITH BUTTER-BEAN MASH AND FRESH MINT SAUCE

Serves 4

If you've never tried butter-bean mash, you're in for a real treat here. Lighter than mashed potato, it's the perfect accompaniment to a summer lamb lunch.

8 lamb cutlets
olive oil, for rubbing
100g watercress
sea salt and freshly ground
    black pepper

FOR THE BUTTER-
BEAN MASH
1 lemon
4 tbsp olive oil
2 × 400g tins butter beans,
    drained and rinsed
50g butter
1 tsp garlic paste
a pinch of sea salt

FOR THE FRESH
MINT SAUCE
a large handful of
    mint leaves
2 tbsp white wine vinegar
½ tsp caster sugar
a pinch of sea salt

To make the butter-bean mash, pare wide strips of zest from the lemon using a vegetable peeler. Be careful not to pick up any of the white pith. Put the zest in a saucepan and add the olive oil. Warm it gently to infuse the lemon into the oil. Leave it to stand while you prep the mint sauce and beans.

To make the mint sauce, put the mint leaves in a mortar and add the vinegar, sugar and a pinch of salt. Pound with a pestle until you have a sauce. Tip into a bowl and put to one side.

Squeeze the juice from the pared lemon into a cup. Put the butter beans in a saucepan and just cover with cold water. Warm them over a low heat to heat through and soften them. Drain them and add the butter, the lemon juice and a good pinch of salt to taste. Add 2 tablespoons of the lemon-infused oil and mash together to a chunky purée.

Rub the lamb cutlets with oil and season with salt and pepper. Get a heavy-based frying pan really hot over a high heat and sear the cutlets for 2 minutes on the first side. Pull the pan from the heat, turn the cutlets over and cook the other side using the heat of the pan for a further 2½ minutes.

Serve the cutlets on top of the bean mash with the watercress alongside. Drizzle over the remaining lemon oil and serve the lamb with the mint sauce.

RED-HOT PEA FALAFELS

Serves 4

Here's one for the chilli lovers – these falafels are a delicious assault on the mouth! Dip into the atomic pepper relish first and enjoy the heat before dipping into the cool cucumber.

2 × 400g tins chickpeas, drained and rinsed
250g frozen peas, defrosted
zest and juice of 1 lemon
50g piece of fresh root ginger, peeled and grated
1 tbsp ground cumin
80g plain flour, plus extra for dusting
sunflower oil, for deep-frying
sea salt

FOR THE COOL CUCUMBER DIP
250g Greek yogurt
½ cucumber, coarsely grated or finely chopped
a large handful of mint leaves, chopped
1 tbsp lemon juice
a large pinch of sea salt

FOR THE ATOMIC PEPPER RELISH
2 red peppers, halved and deseeded
1 tbsp sunflower oil
4 red bird's eye chillies, stalks removed
3 garlic cloves, unpeeled
8 cherry tomatoes
1 tbsp lemon juice
1 tsp honey
1½ tsp sea salt

Preheat the oven to 200°C (180°C fan oven) gas mark 6. To make the cucumber dip, stir all the ingredients together in a bowl. Chill in the fridge until ready to serve.

To make the pepper relish, put the peppers in a roasting tin and drizzle over half the oil. Roast for 10 minutes, then take the tin out of the oven and add the chillies, garlic and tomatoes. Roast for another 10 minutes. Peel the skin from the peppers and remove the garlic skin. Finely chop or use a food processor to blend the roasted ingredients together until you have a chunky paste. Finally, add the lemon juice, honey and salt, and give it one last blitz.

Put the chickpeas and peas in a food processor and blitz until broken down and well combined. Mix in the lemon zest, ginger, cumin, 1 tablespoon salt and about two-thirds of the flour. The mixture should roll into balls, but if it's still too wet, add the remaining flour. Roll the mixture into balls with floured hands (you should be able to make about 16).

Fill a deep-fryer or a large heavy-based saucepan one-third full with sunflower oil and heat it to 180°C (test by frying a small cube of bread; it should brown in 40 seconds). Fry the falafels in batches for 2 minutes, until golden brown. Drizzle them with the lemon juice and a little sea salt, and serve with the relish and dip.

SMOKED MACKEREL, ORANGE AND BEETROOT SALAD

Colourful and nutrient-rich, this salad is perfect on a warm, autumnal day when mackerel, beetroot and oranges are at their seasonal best.

2 large raw beetroots, unpeeled, washed and leaves trimmed to 3cm
a squeeze of lemon juice
300g waxy potatoes, unpeeled, cut lengthways into 5mm-thick slices
4 smoked mackerel fillets
2 oranges
4 tbsp light olive oil
2 tsp wholegrain mustard
80g watercress
8 basil leaves
sea salt and freshly ground black pepper

Put the beetroot in a large saucepan with the lemon juice and a good pinch of salt. Bring the water to the boil over a high heat, then reduce the heat and simmer for 35–40 minutes, or until tender throughout and a knife can be inserted easily.

Meanwhile, after the beetroot has been cooking for 20 minutes, start cooking the potatoes. Put them in a saucepan of cold, salted water over a high heat. Bring to the boil, then reduce the heat and simmer gently for 10–12 minutes.

Remove the skin from the mackerel fillets, then cut away a lengthways strip down the middle of the fillets to remove the pin bones and a small amount of the flesh. Put to one side.

Using a sharp knife, cut a thin slice of peel and pith from one end of each orange. Put, cut side down, in a shallow bowl and cut off the peel and pith in strips. Remove any remaining pith. Cut out each orange segment, leaving the membrane behind. Squeeze the remaining juice from the membrane into the bowl.

Whisk the olive oil and mustard into the orange juice. Season, going easy on the salt, as the mackerel will be salty.

When the beetroot is cooked, scrape off the skin using a knife, then slice thinly.

Drain the potatoes and tip them back into the warm pan. Drizzle with a little of the orange dressing.

Put the watercress in a bowl and remove any thick stems. Tear in the basil leaves. Add a tablespoon of the dressing and toss the leaves to coat them lightly in the dressing.

Lay the warm potato and beetroot slices on a platter. Scatter over the dressed leaves and orange segments. Flake the mackerel into large chunks over the top and finish by drizzling with a little more dressing. Serve any remaining dressing on the side.

Allotment Picnic

Sweet green pea Scotch eggs with courgette fries, broad-bean and pea-tip salad and chunky tomato ketchup. A feast to celebrate your allotment success! For perfect Scotch eggs, a 6-minute boil time, followed by an icy refresh, will give you firm whites and weeping soft yolks so that they don't overcook during frying and baking. Ideally, use young beans that don't need peeling for the salad.

Serves 4

6 eggs (I like
    St Ewe or Burford
    Browns for their
    golden yolks)
100g peas, fresh or frozen
2 × 400g tins chickpeas,
    drained and rinsed
25g basil leaves
4 spring onions, chopped
1 tsp sea salt
½ tsp freshly ground black
    pepper
50g plain flour
25ml milk
150g dried breadcrumbs
sunflower oil, for
    deep-frying

To make the ketchup, heat the oil in a saucepan over a medium-low heat. Add the onion and cook for 5 minutes, stirring regularly, until translucent. Add the garlic and chilli, and cook for 2 minutes or until aromatic.

Add the tomatoes and cook for 5 minutes or until they break down. Add the tomato purée, sugar, mace and vinegar and 50ml water, then cook for a further 10 minutes to allow the mixture to thicken. Put to one side to cool.

Bring a pan of water to the boil and boil four of the eggs for 6 minutes. Immediately refresh them in cold water. Peel off the shells under cold running water and put to one side.

Cook the peas in boiling water for 2 minutes and thoroughly drain. Thoroughly drain the chickpeas, then lay them and the peas on kitchen paper to soak up any remaining moisture. You want the mix to be as dry as possible so that the coating doesn't crack when fried.

In a blender or food processor, blitz together the peas, chickpeas, basil and spring onions with the salt and pepper. Divide the pea mixture into four patties.

Prepare three bowls: one with the flour, one with the remaining two eggs whisked with the milk, and one with the breadcrumbs. Preheat the oven to 180°C (160°C fan oven) gas mark 4.

FOR THE CHUNKY
TOMATO KETCHUP
1 tbsp olive oil
1 onion, finely chopped
2 garlic cloves, crushed
1 small red chilli,
    finely chopped
500g cherry tomatoes,
    roughly chopped
1 tbsp tomato purée
2 tbsp brown sugar
½ tsp ground mace
2 tbsp white wine vinegar

FOR THE BROAD-BEAN
AND PEA-TIP SALAD
1kg young broad beans
5 tbsp olive oil
150ml vegetable stock
4 tbsp torn mint leaves
4 tbsp extra-virgin olive oil
juice of 1 lemon
60g pecorino
    cheese, shaved
80g pea tips
sea salt and freshly
    ground black pepper

FOR THE COURGETTE
FRIES
sunflower oil,
    for deep-frying
240ml milk
240g gram flour
8 medium courgettes, cut
    into 3mm-thick fries

Wrap each of the four boiled eggs in a pea patty and roll into balls to make an even coating. Roll each in the bowl of flour, then dip into the egg mixture and roll around so that it is fully coated. Finally, coat each ball evenly in breadcrumbs.

Fill a deep-fryer or a heavy-based saucepan one-third full with oil and heat it to 175°C (test by frying a small cube of bread; it should brown in 40 seconds). Fry the balls individually for 3 minutes each or until golden brown, keeping them moving in the oil to avoid hot spots.

To finish, put the four egg balls onto a baking tray and bake in the oven for 8 minutes until cooked through. Leave to cool slightly.

Now make the salad. Young beans won't need peeling, but if you are using older bigger beans, put them in a saucepan of boiling water and blanch them for 15 seconds, then refresh them in icy water. Drain in a colander, then slip the beans out of their skins.

Heat the olive oil in a frying pan over a medium heat and add the beans and stock. Bring to the boil, then reduce the heat and simmer for 2 minutes or until the beans are done and the liquid has almost evaporated.

Pull the pan off the heat, then drain the beans in a colander and refresh them in a bowl of iced water. Drain them again, then put the beans in a bowl and add the mint leaves, extra-virgin olive oil and lemon juice, and season to taste with salt and pepper. Leave to one side.

To make the courgette fries, reheat the oil in your deep-fryer or saucepan to 180°C (test by frying a small cube of bread; it should brown in 40 seconds). Have two bowls ready, one containing the milk and one with the gram flour. Season the flour with salt and pepper.

Take a handful of courgette fries, dip and roll them in the milk and then dredge them in the seasoned flour. Using a slotted spoon, gently lower them into the hot oil and fry for 1–2 minutes until crisp and golden. Remove with a slotted spoon, season with salt and pepper and repeat until all the fries are cooked. Top the salad with the shaved pecorino and the pea tips. Serve the fries immediately with the Scotch eggs, ketchup and the broad-bean and pea-tip salad.

CARROT FRITTERS WITH MINTED HONEY YOGURT

These tasty fritters can be prepared in advance and briefly second-fried to crisp up when you are ready to serve. They make a great lunch in their own right, and also an ideal starter to the Keralan Monkfish Curry on page 146.

Makes 20

400g red onions, finely
   sliced into strips
300g carrots, grated
2 tbsp chopped
   coriander leaves
1 tbsp cumin seeds
350g gram flour
1 tsp ground turmeric
1 tsp chilli powder
2 tsp garam masala
2 tsp fine sea salt
sunflower oil, for
   deep-frying

FOR THE MINTED
HONEY YOGURT
300g yogurt
1 tbsp honey
2 tbsp chopped mint leaves
1 tsp fine sea salt

To make the minted honey yogurt, simply mix all the ingredients together in a bowl and leave in the fridge until ready to serve.

Put the onions in a bowl and add the carrots and coriander. Mix together, then put to one side.

Put the cumin seeds in a dry pan and toast them over a medium-high heat for 2 minutes or until fragrant and popping.

Put 200g of the gram flour in a bowl and stir in the toasted cumin seeds and the other spices, the salt and 225ml water, then mix to a paste. Stir this paste into the onions and carrots, and combine well. Leave to stand for 15 minutes.

Fill a deep-fryer or a heavy-based saucepan one-third full with oil and heat it to 175°C (test by frying a small cube of bread; it should brown in 40 seconds). Just before cooking, sift the remaining gram flour into the batter mix to thicken it and stir briefly.

Using two soup spoons, scoop up the batter mix and drop it carefully into your hot oil in small batches. Cook for 1–2 minutes until crispy. Take one fritter aside and cut it open to check that the mix in the centre has cooked through. Serve hot, with the yogurt to dip into.

CORNISH SCOTCH EGGS

Makes 6

Hog's pudding (also used in the salad on page 67) is a traditional Cornish sausage. It's quite peppery, so you only need a small amount to add to regular sausagemeat to give it some punch. It goes really well with egg, so this is a great way to enjoy it.

2 tbsp olive oil
1 large onion, finely diced
2 garlic cloves, crushed
9 large eggs
150g hog's pudding,
    removed from its skin
450g sausagemeat
2 tsp chopped thyme leaves
150g plain flour
200g panko breadcrumbs
a small handful of parsley,
    leaves chopped
4 tbsp milk
sunflower oil, for
    deep-frying

Heat the olive oil in a frying pan over a medium heat and fry the onion gently for 5 minutes or until it turns translucent. Add the garlic and fry for 3 minutes or until everything is cooked and tender but not coloured. Leave to cool.

Boil six of the eggs for 6 minutes in water at a rolling boil, then immediately refresh them in cold water to stop them cooking. Peel off the shells under cold running water and put to one side.

Put the hog's pudding in a food processor and add the sausagemeat. Blitz together, then add the thyme and one of the remaining eggs. Blitz together again until everything is well combined.

Divide the mix evenly into six portions (about 100g each) and flatten into patties ready to wrap around the eggs. Set out three bowls, one containing the flour, one the breadcrumbs and one the remaining two eggs beaten together. Add the parsley to the breadcrumbs and mix well. Add the milk to the eggs and beat in lightly.

Coat the boiled eggs with the flour, which will help the meat to bind to them, and wrap the meat patties around the eggs. Then dip in the egg, followed by the breadcrumbs. Next, do a second coat: dip again in the egg and then in the breadcrumbs.

Fill a deep-fryer or a heavy-based saucepan one-third full with oil and heat it to 170°C (test by frying a small cube of bread; it should brown in 40 seconds). Fry the Scotch eggs individually for 4½ minutes or until golden, keeping them moving in the oil to avoid hot spots. Scoop them out and leave to drain on kitchen paper. Leave them to rest for 3 minutes, then serve warm or cold.

SAMPHIRE FRITTATA WITH WARM LEMONY COURGETTE SALAD

Here is a quick veggie supper. Marsh samphire can be foraged here in Roseland in the summer months. It's famously served with fish, but it goes beautifully with eggs too. You can serve the frittata on its own, perhaps with a crisp green salad, but for a more substantial meal it's great with this summery warm salad, packed with seasonal veg.

Serves 4

FOR THE FRITTATA
250g new potatoes, sliced
2 tbsp sunflower oil, for frying
6 large eggs, beaten
50g samphire
a handful of tarragon, leaves finely shredded
100g soft goat's cheese

FOR THE COURGETTE SALAD
150g runner beans, thinly sliced on the diagonal
3 tbsp olive oil
2 shallots, sliced
3 yellow courgettes (or green if you can't find them), halved and cut into chunky slices
2 garlic cloves, finely chopped
6 small vine-ripened tomatoes, halved or quartered if large
2 rounded tbsp chopped oregano leaves
juice of ½ lemon
sea salt and freshly ground black pepper

To make the courgette salad, steam the runner beans for 5 minutes or until tender. Refresh the beans under cold running water and put to one side.

Meanwhile, heat 2 tablespoons of the olive oil in a frying pan over a medium heat and cook the shallots for 5 minutes until softened. Add the courgettes and garlic, and fry for 3 minutes. Stir in the tomatoes, half the oregano and the lemon juice, then reduce the heat slightly and cook for 5 minutes or until the courgettes are just tender but retain a little bite and the tomatoes have started to break down.

Stir in the runner beans, add the remaining olive oil, and season with salt and pepper, then warm through. Keep the salad warm while you make the frittata.

Put the potatoes in a pan of cold salted water and bring to the boil. Cook for 15 minutes or until tender, then drain in a colander. Heat the oil in an ovenproof frying pan. Add the drained potatoes, and the beaten eggs, most of the samphire and the tarragon. Lay the remaining samphire elegantly on the top. Crumble over the goat's cheese and season with salt and pepper (remembering the salty flavour of the samphire, so you won't need much salt).

Preheat your grill. Cook the frittata for 7–10 minutes on the hob over a medium heat, enough to set the bottom, then finish under the grill until just set all the way through. Add the remaining oregano leaves to the salad and serve it warm with the frittata.

BEETROOT BURGERS

These are just as lovely on their own with a salad as they are in a traditional burger bun. They make a great veggie dinner that the whole family will enjoy.

Serves 6

500g raw beetroot, grated
150g carrot, grated
4 spring onions, sliced
2 red chillies, deseeded
    and sliced
400g tin chickpeas,
    drained and rinsed
1 large egg, beaten
100g panko breadcrumbs
1 tbsp chopped mint leaves,
    plus extra to garnish
1 tbsp chopped
    coriander leaves
zest of 1 lemon
1½ tbsp fine sea salt
2 tbsp sunflower oil
6 tbsp natural yogurt,
    to serve

FOR THE QUICK PICKLE
100ml white wine vinegar
75g caster sugar
½ cucumber, halved
    lengthways, deseeded
    and sliced into
    half-moons
1 red onion, thinly sliced
1 tsp fine sea salt

Put the beetroot in a bowl and add the carrot, spring onions and chillies. Put the chickpeas in a food processor and blitz. Add to the bowl, followed by the egg, breadcrumbs, herbs, lemon zest and salt. Mix together until well combined, then leave to rest for 10 minutes to firm up. Preheat the oven to 200°C (180°C fan oven) gas mark 6.

Meanwhile, make the pickle. Put the vinegar and sugar in a small saucepan and bring to the boil over a medium-high heat, then drop in the cucumber and onion. Add the salt. Put to one side while you cook the burgers.

Split the burger mix into six pieces (roughly 180g each) and mould into burgers. Heat a frying pan with the oil over a medium heat and cook the burgers for 1–2 minutes on each side until nicely caramelised (this can be done in batches). Put on a baking tray and cook in the oven for 10 minutes.

Drain the pickle and put it in a serving bowl. Serve each burger with a spoonful of yogurt and the pickle and garnished with mint leaves.

Lemony
Courgettes
and
Halloumi
with
Beetroot,
Chickpeas
and
Hazelnut
Pesto

Lemony Courgettes and Halloumi with Beetroot, Chickpeas and Hazelnut Pesto

This feast is full of the bright flavours of late summer. The courgettes and halloumi have roughly the same cook time, so they are perfect to grill together. If you have access to a barbecue, they will taste amazing cooked over hot coals with rosemary smoke. Replace the Parmesan in the pesto for a vegetarian alternative, if you prefer.

Serves 8

5 tbsp olive oil
thickly pared zest and
	the juice of 4 lemons
3 garlic cloves, peeled
8 courgettes, cut into
	5mm-thick slices
1.2kg halloumi, cut into
	5mm-thick slices
a bunch of mint, leaves
	roughly chopped
sea salt and freshly ground
	black pepper

FOR THE BEETROOT
16 even-sized small raw
	beetroots (1.6kg total
	weight), unpeeled,
	washed and leaves
	trimmed to 3cm
olive oil, for brushing
leaves from 4 thyme sprigs
flaked sea salt and freshly
	ground black pepper

FOR THE PESTO
200g hazelnuts
100g basil leaves
100g Parmesan
	cheese, grated
zest and juice of 2 lemons
400ml extra-virgin olive oil
2 tsp flaked sea salt
4 garlic cloves, peeled
	and left whole

FOR THE CHICKPEAS
4 × 400g tins chickpeas,
	drained and rinsed
	thoroughly
4 tbsp olive oil, for roasting
4 tbsp finely chopped
	rosemary leaves, plus
	extra for sprinkling
1 tbsp sea salt
2 tsp garlic powder
2 tbsp soft brown sugar

Preheat the oven to 200°C (180°C fan oven) gas mark 6. To prepare the beetroot, put the beets in a large roasting tin, then brush or roll them in olive oil so that they are well covered. Sprinkle with sea salt and the thyme leaves.

Cook in the oven for 1 hour or until the beets are soft and cooked through. Remove the tin from the oven, then leave the beets to cool. Once cooled, rub the skins away using a piece of kitchen paper – they should come away easily. Be careful of the beetroot juice while doing this, as it can stain clothing. Cut away the root and stalks, and chop the beets into 5cm chunks. Season with salt and pepper to taste and set aside until ready to serve.

Reduce the oven temperature to 190°C (170°C fan oven) gas mark 5. Spread the hazelnuts for the pesto over a baking tray and cook in the oven for 7–10 minutes until the skins have darkened and the nuts are golden underneath. Rub the nuts between two clean tea towels to loosen the skins. Pick the hazelnuts out from the skins. Blitz these in a blender or food processor, along with the other pesto ingredients. Pour into a serving bowl and put to one side.

To prepare the chickpeas, dry the chickpeas using kitchen paper, then put them in a bowl and toss them with the olive oil. Add the remaining ingredients and stir to coat evenly. Spread out the coated chickpeas on the baking tray and roast for 20 minutes or until just starting to turn golden and crispy. Sprinkle with flaked salt and rosemary leaves, and put to one side in a serving dish.

To cook the courgettes and halloumi, heat the olive oil in a frying pan over a medium heat and add the strips of lemon zest and the garlic. Bring to a simmer and then remove from the heat and set aside to allow the flavours to infuse the oil.

Preheat a griddle pan or a barbecue grill rack until it's really hot. Once you have done this, you can discard the garlic cloves and zest from the resting infused oil. Add the lemon juice to the infused oil and dip in the courgette and halloumi slices. Cook the slices for 2–3 minutes on each side until charred and tender. Sprinkle with fresh mint and season with salt and pepper. Serve with the chickpeas, beetroot and pesto.

Supper is the most celebrated meal at the Hidden Hut. It happens only once a week and takes days of planning and preparation. We call these suppers 'feast nights'.

Whether you cook on a wood-fired grill in the garden or a hob in the kitchen, there are ideas here that will enable you to make the most of where you are and draw people together through good food. It doesn't always have to be an impressive spread: sometimes just a bowl of slow beef ragù and pasta is the right for the occasion, while other evenings may call for a lavish seafood paella cooked over a fire pit, if you have one. It's about an offering of food that makes people feel welcome and wanting to stick around for more.

3

Dusk

TARRAGON-CRUMBED SOLE WITH TWICE-COOKED CHIPS

With a delicate fish like lemon sole you want to keep the flavours simple. Soft herbs such as tarragon work beautifully. Twice-cooking the chips gives you really light, fluffy chips that are crispy without being burnt. The potatoes are first blanched to soften them. Then the second cooking on a higher heat is to crisp the outer layer.

Serves 4

juice of ½ orange
a handful of tarragon
   leaves, chopped
2 tbsp Dijon mustard
200ml crème fraîche
150g fresh white
   breadcrumbs
2 tbsp plain flour
4 lemon sole fillets,
   skinned
4 tbsp sunflower oil
sea salt and freshly
   ground black
   pepper
crushed minted
   peas, to serve

FOR THE TWICE-COOKED CHIPS
1.2kg potatoes for
   chips (ideally Maris
   Piper), unpeeled,
   scrubbed, and cut
   into thin chips
sunflower oil, for
   deep-frying
flaked sea salt

Using a mortar and pestle, grind together ½ teaspoon salt with the orange juice and tarragon. In a bowl, mix together the mustard and crème fraîche and then add the tarragon mixture.

Line a baking tray with baking parchment. Put the breadcrumbs in one large bowl and the flour in another. Season the flour with salt and pepper. Dust the fish fillets in the flour, shaking off the excess. Spread the herby mustard crème fraîche over one side of each fillet, then firmly press into the breadcrumbs. Lay the fish on the prepared baking tray, crumb side up, and chill in the fridge while you prepare the chips.

Preheat the oven to 110°C (90°C fan oven) gas mark ¼ and put a baking tray in the oven to warm. Rinse the chips in cold water as soon as you have cut them, then drain and pat dry. Fill a deep-fryer or a large saucepan one-third full with oil and heat it to 150°C (test by frying a small cube of bread; it should brown in 60 seconds). Fry the chips in small batches for 8 minutes until tender, remove from the oil and put to one side.

Increase the heat of the oil to 190°C (test by frying a small cube of bread; it should brown in 20 seconds) and cook the chips again, this time for 2–3 minutes or until crispy and golden. Season with some flaked sea salt and keep the chips warm on the baking tray in the oven until ready to serve.

Add the 4 tablespoons of sunflower oil to a frying pan and heat until sizzling hot. Add the crumbed fish in batches and cook for 2 minutes on each side or until cooked through. Serve with the chips, some crushed minted peas and lemon wedges.

WHOLE BAKED TURBOT WITH TENDERSTEM BROCCOLI AND POTATO GALETTE

Turbot is known locally as the 'king of the sea'. Serve this fish in the centre of the table to allow everyone to get stuck in. By baking the fish whole, you retain the sought-after flavours from the turbot's bones. The buttery cooking juices, with hints of lemon and bay leaf, make a delicious dressing for the broccoli.

Serves 4

1 turbot, gills and tail
   trimmed
5 bay leaves
olive oil, for drizzling
juice of 1 lemon
100g butter, softened,
   in small lumps
a small bunch of tarragon,
   leaves chopped

FOR THE POTATO GALETTE
125g butter
3 tbsp chopped
   thyme leaves
1kg potatoes, (ideally Maris
   Piper) peeled and finely
   sliced
sea salt and freshly
   ground black pepper

FOR THE CHARRED BROCCOLI
a handful of mixed seeds,
   such as pumpkin
   and sunflower
400g Tenderstem broccoli

To make the galette, preheat the oven to 200°C (180°C fan oven) gas mark 6. Put a quarter of the butter into a heavy-based ovenproof frying pan, then heat over a medium heat until just melted. Take off the heat and add a pinch of the thyme leaves, then arrange the potatoes in circular layers in the pan, seasoning with salt, pepper and thyme at every layer.

Dot the remaining butter on top of the galette, then bake for 45 minutes – removing the pan from the oven every 10 minutes and pressing the potato down firmly using a plate. Wrap in foil to keep warm until ready to serve.

Turn the oven temperature up to 240°C (220°C fan oven) gas mark 9 and place a large baking tray inside to heat up. Put the turbot on a chopping board, dark side up, and score 5 diagonal slashes heavily across the skin. Fold the bay leaves lengthways and insert them into the slashes.

Once the tray is burning hot, remove from the oven and drizzle it with oil. Put the fish on the tray and squeeze over the lemon juice, then add another drizzle of oil and a good scattering of salt over the top. Put the fish in the oven and roast for 20 minutes.

To cook the broccoli, first put the seeds in a dry frying pan and toast them over a medium-high heat for 2 minutes or until golden. Put to one side.

Increase the heat of the frying pan until really hot. Cook the broccoli in the pan for 2 minutes, turning them until charred and tender. Set aside and keep warm.

Once the turbot is out of the oven, scatter the butter over the fish and leave it to melt then sprinkle over the tarragon. Pour the turbot butter from the roasting dish over the charred broccoli and scatter with the toasted seeds. Pour off the excess butter from the galette and transfer it from the pan onto a serving dish.

The best way to eat the turbot is to use a blunt knife to gently ease the flesh away from the frame (bones), top layer first, then once that has all gone, pick up the fish by the tail and turn it over to do the same with the underside. You can eat the skin or discard it – that's totally up to you. Serve with the galette and broccoli.

PORTSCATHO FISH PIE

This pie has become a Good Friday tradition at the hut. It is nearly always our first feast of the year, and there's nothing more fitting than a creamy fish and potato pie. It marks the start of the season for us. This is our tried-and-tested recipe, scaled down.

Serves 4–6

100g butter
100g plain flour
900ml whole milk
100ml double cream
2 tbsp Dijon mustard
2 tbsp chopped tarragon
    leaves
2 tbsp chopped parsley
    leaves
1 tbsp chopped dill fronds
1 tbsp Worcestershire
    sauce
juice of 2 lemons
2 tsp sea salt
1 tsp freshly ground
    black pepper
800g skinless, boneless
    Cornish pollock, cut
    into chunks
3 large eggs
100g samphire

FOR THE TOPPING
1.2kg potatoes (such
    as Maris Piper), peeled
    and chopped
2 tbsp Dijon mustard
2 tsp freshly ground
    black pepper
300g Cornish Cheddar
    cheese (such as Cornish
    Davidstow), grated
100g fresh white
    breadcrumbs
sea salt

Melt the butter in a large pan over a medium heat and add the flour, then gently cook for 1 minute, stirring. Gradually add the milk, little by little, stirring the whole time. Add the double cream and continue stirring.

Add the Dijon mustard, chopped herbs, Worcestershire sauce and lemon juice. Season with the salt and pepper, and cook over a medium heat for 1 minute. Add the fish, mix gently and then pour into an ovenproof dish. Leave aside to cool.

Cook the eggs in boiling water for 10 minutes, then refresh under cold water, peel off the shells while held under the tap, and cut the eggs in half. Place on top of the fish pie mix in the dish and add the samphire.

To make the topping, put the potatoes in cold salted water and bring to the boil. Cook for 20 minutes or until tender. Drain and mash, adding the mustard, pepper and 2 teaspoons salt. Preheat the oven to 200°C (180°C fan oven) gas mark 6.

Spoon the mash evenly over the fish mixture, then top with the grated cheese and the breadcrumbs. Bake in the oven for 25 minutes until golden, then serve.

145　Dusk

KERALAN MONKFISH CURRY

Cornish monkfish lends itself really well to curries and sauce-based dishes. Its firm, meaty texture holds really well and doesn't break down, so you get lovely chunks of curried monkfish fillet with each serving. It has a naturally mild flavour, so it is also a great choice for people who aren't keen on 'fishy' fish.

Serves 4

4 monkfish fillets
(about 170g each),
membrane
removed, cut into
3cm chunks
juice of 2 limes
2 tsp ground turmeric
1 tsp cayenne pepper
½ tsp fenugreek seeds
2 tsp coriander seeds
1 tbsp coconut oil
or sunflower oil
2 tsp mustard seeds
20 curry leaves
2 onions, finely
chopped
200g cherry tomatoes
1 tbsp tomato purée
2 red chillies, deseeded
and roughly
chopped
1cm piece of fresh root
ginger, peeled and
grated
3 garlic cloves, peeled
1 mango, peeled and
roughly chopped
2 tsp tamarind paste
250ml coconut milk
sea salt

TO SERVE
200g coconut cream
1 green chilli, deseeded
and finely chopped
a handful of coriander,
leaves finely chopped
steamed basmati rice

Put the monkfish in a bowl and add the lime juice, turmeric and cayenne pepper, then season with salt. Leave to chill in the fridge while you prepare the curry base.

In a dry frying pan over a medium heat, toast the fenugreek and coriander seeds for 1–2 minutes until they start to crackle and release their flavour. Tip them into a mortar and grind with a pestle. Put to one side.

In the same pan, heat the coconut oil and fry the mustard seeds and curry leaves for 1–2 minutes, until the seeds start to crackle. Add the onions, along with a pinch of salt and the ground coriander and fenugreek seeds from the mortar. Cook gently for 5–8 minutes until the onions have softened and turned translucent.

While the onions and spices are cooking, put the cherry tomatoes into a blender and add the tomato purée, red chillies, ginger, garlic, mango and tamarind paste, and whizz until smooth. Pour this mixture and the coconut milk into the pan with the onions, and stir well. Bring to the boil, then reduce the heat and simmer for 5 minutes.

Gently add the marinated monkfish chunks, stirring them in carefully, and let them cook in the sauce for 4–6 minutes until just cooked – be careful about overcooking them, or they will turn tough.

Let the curry sit for a few minutes off the heat. Serve topped with a spoonful of coconut cream, the chopped green chilli and coriander leaves and with a steaming bowl of basmati rice.

GURNARD STEW

A wholesome pot of gurnard stew, served in the middle of the table with a dish of aioli and a loaf of sourdough to soak up the broth, is so good that it will leave you going back for more. Gurnard is the fish I most associate with Cornish seafood stews. It's got everything going for it: colour, flavour and a robust texture.

Serves 4

2 tbsp olive oil
2 onions, sliced
4 celery sticks, sliced
1 fennel bulb, sliced
2 garlic cloves, sliced
150ml white wine
a pinch of saffron threads
400g tin chopped tomatoes
450ml fish stock
75g wild garlic
    leaves, chopped
400g skinless gurnard
    fillet, cut into 3cm
    chunks
1kg mussels, cleaned
    (see page 158)
sea salt and freshly
    ground black pepper
aioli (see page 90) and
    sourdough bread,
    to serve

Heat the oil in a large saucepan over a low heat and sweat the veg and garlic for 5 minutes. Add the wine and saffron, and turn the heat up to medium. Bring to the boil, then reduce the heat and simmer until reduced by a half.

Add the tomatoes and stock, then bring back to the boil, reduce the heat and simmer for 15 minutes.

Add the wild garlic, and mix in, then add the gurnard and mussels. Stir, then cover with a lid and simmer for 5 minutes or until the mussels have opened. Discard any that haven't opened. Check the seasoning (the mussels give a salty flavour to the dish) and add salt and pepper to taste. Serve with aioli and sourdough bread.

Feast nights at the Hidden Hut

What started almost a decade ago as an ad hoc mackerel grill advertised by a blackboard on the road has turned into an annual calendar of wood-fired feast nights – from salt-baked lamb to lobster and chips. One dish is served per night and you buy a ticket for the night you wish to come to. The whole family is welcome. You bring your own plates, cutlery and drinks, and get stuck in. The nights are very Cornish in their laid-back vibe. For us, each feast takes days of preparation, from building the grills and chopping the firewood to washing the blankets and prepping the produce that comes direct from the boats and fields. It's a labour of love, and we really do love it. They are our favourite night of the week.

At the start of every season, usually early February, I gather our whole team together around the kitchen table with a huge wall planner and we map out our feast calendar for the year. This can drag on long into the evening as we all bring our thoughts and ideas to the table. It's not as simple as just writing a menu. The feasts are entirely outdoors, in all weathers. The food is cooked over wood fires and served in one hit. There are so many unusual considerations that need to be taken into account. What type of wood should we use to cook a brisket of beef over? Do we have a pan big enough to cook potato rösti for 100? Will watercress leaves get blown off people's plates if it's windy? We usually go through about seven pots of coffee.

Come Easter, the first feast is upon us. Week by week from then on, the feast nights come round thick and fast and we work hard to deliver what we have promised, whether it's balmy and calm or thrashing down with an easterly. Every year, we always think we've grown wise enough to prepare for every eventuality. But each year, without fail, something always crops up and knocks us for six. We've had storms, power cuts, wet log deliveries, cliff erosions and local sardine shortages. But we've never had to cancel a single feast.

There's always been a way. Even if that's involved picking up the hut with a crane and moving it back 10 metres after a storm. If it can be done, it will get done!

For me, one of the best things about cooking over fire and eating outdoors is the theatrics involved and the atmosphere it creates. The wood fires transform the cooking area into the centre of the party. Everyone is waiting and watching the same food being transformed from fresh produce to a finished dish. It's a sensory experience and creates an atmosphere of togetherness and anticipation. I love it that people feel a part of the process. They leave talking not just about the food, but about the whole experience.

Each feast night is different and memorable in its own way. We are lucky that we get a real eclectic mix of people coming to our nights. All of them have been through the same tense booking process a few weeks before, and all have found their way to the hut that night through the country lanes and fields, all for the same reason. However, each person brings something unique to the table, be it a story to tell, a rare whisky to share or an ornate candelabra. Even when the clouds are grey and the local dolphins are nowhere to be seen, the place feels magical and alive – and that's as much due to the feasters as it is to our fires and food.

Seafood Paella
for 40

This is the ultimate showboat feast. It's relatively simple to do, as you can cook all 40 portions in one huge pan. It's a great way to feed a crowd and to showcase local seafood.

You'll need a 90cm paella pan, a 20-litre stock pan and a gas burner with a stand – or just the pans and a heatproof stand if you're cooking it wild over a wood fire, like I do at the hut. If you're cooking outdoors, you'll need to make sure your pan is absolutely level. Use a spirit level, if you have one. If not, do it by eye using a bowl of water. This is really important to ensure the paella cooks evenly throughout.

The shellfish needs to be cleaned. Scrub the clams thoroughly in cold running water and prepare the mussels as explained on page 158. Discard any shells that remain open after being sharply tapped.

First, you need to make a great fish stock. There is no point in spending a fortune on lavish seafood if your stock is weak. I always start my stocks with a turbot frame (bones), which you can usually source quite easily from a good fishmonger.

Serves 40

500ml olive oil
3kg onions, diced
6 fennel bulbs, sliced
5 garlic cloves, crushed
75cl bottle white wine
3kg squid tubes, sliced
    into rings, plus tentacles
3kg mussels, cleaned
    as page 158
2kg cockles, cleaned
    as above
2kg clams, cleaned
    as above
2 tbsp smoked paprika
3 tbsp tomato purée
5kg bomba rice
3kg white fish fillets,
skinned and pin-boned (see
    page 55)
1kg cooked crab claws
4 bunches of soft herbs,
    such as parsley, chives,
    chervil or tarragon,
    leaves chopped
10 lemons, cut into quarters
aioli (see page 90) and
    wild rocket, to serve

FOR THE FISH STOCK

5kg turbot frames (bones),
    washed and trimmed
1 bay leaf
2 onions, roughly chopped
5 garlic cloves, peeled
10 black peppercorns
2 tbsp sea salt
2 leeks, roughly chopped
5 carrots, roughly chopped
2 tsp saffron threads
3 tbsp paprika

To make the stock, put the turbot frames in a 20-litre stock pan and add the bay leaf, onions, garlic, peppercorns, 1 tablespoon of the salt, the leeks and carrots. Cover with cold water to fill two-thirds of the pan. Bring the liquid to the boil then reduce the heat and simmer for 30 minutes. Remove the turbot frames with tongs and strain the liquid into a clean saucepan using a sieve.

Measure the liquid and make it up to 14 litres with fresh water. Add the saffron, paprika and the remaining 1 tablespoon salt. When ready to cook the paella, bring the stock back up to the boil.

Using a 90cm paella pan, heat the oil over a medium heat and cook the onions and fennel for 4 minutes. Then add the garlic and wine and stir to deglaze the pan to pick up the onion and fennel flavours.

Add the squid rings and tentacles to the pan, and simmer for 1 minute, then add all the shellfish (mussels, cockles and clams). These will open up and leach their juices into the pan. Cook now on quite a high heat for another 3 minutes to reduce those juices and evaporate any water. Unlike cooking paella at home in the oven, here you add the shellfish earlier on to ensure they are cooked through and allow their juices to infuse the rice.

Now add the smoked paprika and tomato purée, and give the mixture a good stir to coat everything, then pour over your 14 litres of boiling fish stock. Bring back up to an even simmer and add the rice, pouring it evenly over the pan. Stir in and level the rice off, then leave the pan well alone.

The cooking time depends on a number of variables: wind speed, outside temperature, cooking method (gas or wood), and so on. But as a guide, cook over a high heat for 15 minutes. Do not stir after the rice has been added.

After the high-heat cooking, drop the temperature right down to a light simmer. Lay the fish fillets on top of the paella and submerge them by pushing them gently with the back of a spoon. Cook for a further 15–20 minutes over a low heat until all the stock has been absorbed into the rice. After 10 minutes, dig the crab claws in so that the pincers are pointing upwards – in this way they can heat through.

Once cooked, take the pan off the heat and garnish with fresh soft herbs and lemon wedges. It's nice if the paella can stand for 5 minutes to allow it to rest before serving. Serve with aioli and wild rocket, and have a claw cracker, pick and fork to use to eat the seafood. One of the best bits is the dark crunchy rice on the base of the pan – don't make the mistake of discarding it.

SCALLOP RISOTTO

Caramelising the scallops on a hot griddle intensifies their sweetness, creating this richly flavoured scallop and summer-vegetable risotto. The griddling in this recipe contrasts with the slow, braised flavours and textures of the risotto. It's definitely worth the extra washing-up.

Serves 4

800ml hot chicken stock
2 tbsp olive oil
100g butter
1 fennel bulb, diced
2 onions, diced
4 garlic cloves, crushed
1 bay leaf
400g risotto rice
200ml white wine
40g Parmesan
   cheese, grated
1 tbsp mascarpone
2 tbsp finely chopped
   parsley
16 large scallops, corals
   discarded if you prefer
2 lemons, halved

FOR THE DRESSING
3 tbsp chopped parsley
3 tbsp chopped basil
juice of 2 lemons
150ml extra-virgin olive oil
sea salt and freshly
   ground black pepper

FOR THE GRILLED VEG
1 green courgette, cut
   lengthways and sliced
   into half-moons
   1cm thick
1 yellow courgette,
   cut lengthways and
   sliced into half-moons
   1cm thick
12 cherry tomatoes on
   the vine
1 tbsp olive oil

Keep the stock simmering in a saucepan while you make the risotto. Heat the olive oil and half the butter in a large saucepan over a medium heat and cook the fennel, onions and garlic for 5 minutes or until softened but not coloured.

Add the bay leaf and rice, and cook for 2 minutes, stirring. Add the wine, raise the heat and simmer until it has all evaporated, then add three-quarters of the hot chicken stock, one ladleful at a time, stirring constantly with a wooden spoon and waiting until each ladleful is absorbed before adding the next. This will take about 20 minutes.

To make the dressing, put the parsley in a small bowl and add the basil, lemon juice and oil, season and whisk well to combine.

To make the grilled veg, put the courgettes and tomatoes in a clean bowl and coat with the oil. Heat a griddle pan over a high heat. Season the veg and cook in the griddle for 1 minute on each side. Transfer to a bowl and add 1 tablespoon of the herby dressing, then put to one side.

Add the remaining stock to the risotto, a ladleful at a time, stirring as before, until the rice is tender but still has a bite. Finish by stirring in the Parmesan, mascarpone, parsley and the remaining butter, stirring vigorously. Cover with a lid and leave to rest, off the heat, while cooking the scallops.

Heat the griddle pan to high and season the scallops generously. Cook on the hot griddle for 90 seconds on each side, adding the corals, if using, while cooking the second side, then add the lemon halves, cut side down, to lightly caramelise at the same time. To serve, divide the risotto between plates, put the scallops on top and serve with the courgettes and tomatoes. Drizzle generously with the herby dressing.

156 Dusk

KING HARRY MUSSELS, THREE WAYS

The Hidden Hut is located on a peninsula called the Roseland. It sometimes feels like an island because you have to get the King Harry Ferry across the River Fal to reach the 'mainland' where the nearest towns and shops are. Just next to the King Harry Ferry is a fantastic local mussel farm.

This recipe is a celebration of this local delicacy. Steaming is the most common way to cook mussels, but here are a few ideas for baking and grilling them too.

For each recipe, first you need to prepare the mussels. Scrub the mussel shells with a stiff brush and rinse under cold running water. Discard any mussels that remain open after being sharply tapped. Scrape off any barnacles and remove the beards with a small knife. Rinse well.

Each recipe serves 4

BAKED MUSSELS WITH FENNEL AND LEEK

2 leeks, sliced
2 fennel bulbs, sliced
60ml olive oil
½ tsp sea salt
1 tsp fennel seeds
1.5kg mussels, cleaned
   as above
100ml Pernod or pastis
300ml fish stock (see
   page 153)
150g butter, diced
50g tarragon
   leaves, chopped

Preheat the oven to 220°C (200°C fan oven) gas mark 7. Put the leeks and fennel in a large roasting tin. Add the oil, salt and fennel seeds, then bake for 10 minutes or until the vegetables are softening.

Add the mussels and bake for 5 minutes more. Add the Pernod, stock and butter, and cook in the oven for another 3 minutes. Discard any mussels that haven't opened. Stir in the tarragon and serve.

GRILLED MUSSELS WITH BEER, BACON AND THYME

50g butter
2 tbsp olive oil
8 rashers of smoked
    bacon, chopped
5 garlic cloves, chopped
100g thyme sprigs
200ml chicken stock
500ml beer
1 tbsp wholegrain mustard
1 tbsp light brown sugar
juice of ½ lemon
200ml double cream
1.5kg mussels, cleaned
    as on page 158

Prepare and heat up your barbecue. Heat the butter and oil in a saucepan over a medium-high heat and, when the butter has melted, cook the bacon for 4 minutes until crispy. Add the garlic and thyme, and cook for 1 minute, then add the stock, beer, mustard and sugar. Bring to the boil and cook for 1 minute, then add the lemon juice and cream. Stir and put to one side.

Meanwhile, grill the mussels on the barbecue grill rack until just starting to open, then transfer to the saucepan and cook for 1 minute over a medium heat. Discard any mussels that haven't opened, and serve. (Alternatively, cook the mussels in the pan: add them with the garlic and thyme, then cover the pan with a lid and cook for 2 minutes or until they are open.)

STEAMED MUSSELS WITH SAMPHIRE, GARLIC AND WINE

50g butter
2 tbsp olive oil
3 onions, sliced
10 garlic cloves,
    roughly chopped
3 bay leaves
1.5kg mussels, cleaned
    as on page 158
600ml white wine
200g samphire
200ml double cream
75g parsley
    leaves, chopped
juice of ½ lemon
½ tsp freshly ground
    black pepper
sea salt

Heat the butter and oil in a large saucepan over a medium heat and sweat the onions, garlic and bay leaves until softened but not coloured.

Add the mussels and the white wine, cover with a lid and bring to the boil. Cook for 3 minutes over a high heat until all the mussels have opened – discard any that haven't.

Add the samphire and cream, and cook for 1 more minute, then add the parsley, lemon juice and pepper. Taste and add salt if it needs it (it will depend on how salty the mussels and samphire are). Serve.

CRAB CRUMBLE

In winter, crabs are not only cheaper to buy than in the summer, but they are also much richer in the lovely brown meat, which makes this dish so rich and flavoursome.

If you're using whole crabs, two will give you about the right amount of crab meat for this recipe.

Serves 4

1 onion, halved
2 cloves
4 black peppercorns
2 bay leaves
200ml whole milk
200ml single cream
100g unsalted butter
60g plain flour
400g cooked white crab
    meat, flaked
200g cooked brown crab
    meat, flaked
1 tbsp finely chopped
    tarragon leaves
2 tsp mustard powder
3 large egg yolks, beaten
juice of 1 lemon
Worcestershire sauce
sea salt and freshly
    ground black pepper
soft chopped herbs, such
    as parsley, chives,
    chervil or tarragon, to
    garnish

**FOR THE
CRUMBLE TOPPING**
100g plain flour
50g ground almonds
50g Parmesan
    cheese, grated
50g butter, softened
    and diced

To make the crumble topping, put the flour in a large bowl and add the ground almonds and grated Parmesan. Mix well, then rub the butter into the flour mixture using your fingertips until it starts to resemble breadcrumbs. Leave aside while you make the filling.

Put the onion in a small saucepan and add the cloves, peppercorns, bay leaves, milk and cream. Bring to the boil over a medium-high heat, then remove from the heat, cover and leave to infuse for 15 minutes. Strain into a jug. Preheat the oven to 220°C (200°C fan oven) gas mark 7.

Rinse out the milk pan, then melt half the butter over a low heat. Using a wooden spoon, stir in the flour and cook for 1 minute, then slowly add the strained milk, stirring all the time to form a smooth sauce. Cook gently for 2–3 minutes, stirring regularly, until thickened, then remove from the heat.

Add the white and brown crab meat to the sauce, along with the tarragon, mustard powder, egg yolks, lemon juice and a few drops of Worcestershire sauce. Season with salt and pepper.

Spoon the crab mixture into an ovenproof dish and cover with the crumble mix. Dot with the remaining butter. Bake for 25–30 minutes until golden. Garnish with soft herbs and serve.

Wood-
Fired
Lobster
and
Rosemary
Sea-Salted
Chips

Wood-Fired Lobster and Rosemary Sea-Salted Chips

Lobster and chips is our most iconic feast-night meal. Here is a scaled-down version for you to cook at home for your friends and family. If you get to pick a live lobster at your local fish seller, go for the gnarliest one you can find. This will mean that it hasn't shed its shell recently, so it will have the best flavour.

Thanks to the amazing work of the National Lobster Hatchery in Padstow, wild lobster stocks are once again strong around Cornwall. It's a brilliant local project that operates a buy one, set one free scheme to ensure the long-term sustainability of these magnificent creatures.

Serves 8

4 live cold-water lobsters (about 1.2–1.4kg each)
butter, for cooking
watercress and lemon wedges, to serve

FOR THE TARRAGON DRESSING
2 tsp Dijon mustard
1 tbsp cider vinegar
½ tsp caster sugar
200ml light olive oil
juice of 1 lemon
2 tbsp chopped tarragon leaves
sea salt and freshly ground black pepper

FOR THE ROSEMARY SEA SALT
100g fine sea salt
25g rosemary leaves

FOR THE CHIPS
1.6kg potatoes (ideally Maris Piper), cut into thin chips
sunflower oil, for deep-frying

Put your live lobsters into a freezer for 30 minutes to sedate them. Meanwhile, make the tarragon dressing. In a mixing bowl, whisk the mustard, vinegar and sugar together. Then slowly pour in the oil in a steady stream, whisking all the time. Add 75ml water and the lemon juice and tarragon, season with salt and pepper and whisk to a smooth emulsion. Put into a serving bowl and set aside.

Next, make the rosemary salt. Blitz the salt and rosemary together in a blender until fine and a light green colour. Put to one side in an open bowl.

Bring a large pan of salted water to the boil. Take a lobster out of the freezer. Lay it flat, stomach side down, on a chopping board. Spike it firmly and quickly with a large sharp knife in the base of its head and swiftly cut straight down. Place it in the boiling water and cook for 8 minutes, then refresh in cold water. Repeat with the other lobsters.

To cook the chips, rinse the potatoes in cold water as soon as you have cut them, then drain and pat dry on kitchen paper. Fill a deep-fryer or a large saucepan one-third full with oil and heat it to 150°C (test by frying a small cube of bread; it should brown in 60 seconds). Fry the chips in small batches for 8 minutes until tender, remove from the oil and put to one side (this is the first cooking).

Now prep the lobsters as explained on page 60. The lobsters are now ready to be cooked a second time. They can be cooked on the barbecue to infuse with a smokey flavour (shell side down to preserve the juices in the meat) or in the oven at 200°C (180°C fan oven) gas mark 6. If using a wood fire, cook over a medium heat – that's when you can hold your hand comfortably over the grill for 5–6 seconds. The wood coals should be glowing and covered in white ash. Cook in either of these ways for 8 minutes, dotted with some butter.

While the lobsters are cooking, refry your chips. Increase the heat of the oil to 190°C (test by frying a small cube of bread; it should brown in 20 seconds) and cook the chips again, this time for 2–3 minutes or until crispy and golden. Drain and season with the rosemary salt.

Serve the cooked lobster with the rosemary chips, a good spoonful of the tarragon dressing, some watercress and a big wedge of lemon.

GRILLED PORK AND STONE FRUIT WITH BURRATA

If you've fired up a wood grill, make this simple, but memorable, lunch. Using wood will give you a softer, smokier heat than charcoal for grilling the pork and delicate stone fruits. I also like to throw a few branches of rosemary onto the hot wood coals to give the smoke a great flavour.

You'll need to arrange the embers in your grill so that you leave an area where you don't have any direct heat, in other words, an ember-free area (see page 78 for more on this).

Serves 4

4 centre-cut loin
    pork chops
juice of 1 lemon
4 small thyme sprigs and
    the leaves of 2 sprigs
4 rashers of Parma ham
2 very ripe peaches, pitted
    and cut in half
2 very ripe nectarines,
    pitted and cut
    in half
2 very ripe apricots, pitted
    and cut in half
olive oil, for brushing
60g pine nuts
500g burrata di bufala
    or buffalo mozzarella
extra-virgin olive oil,
    for drizzling
a bunch of fresh basil,
    leaves torn
a bunch of fresh mint,
    leaves finely chopped
flaked sea salt and freshly
    ground black pepper

Where the embers are, you want a flame-free even heat at a temperature where you can hold your hand comfortably over the grill for 3–4 seconds. Sear the pork over the direct heat of the embers on the hottest part of the grill for 2 minutes on each side, then move them over to the ember-free area of the grill.

Squeeze the lemon juice over the pork chops, and add salt, pepper and the thyme sprigs. Put the ham over the hot area of the grill for 20 seconds or until wilted and lightly crisp. Peel off the ham and drape it over the pork chops. Let the chops cook through gently over the low heat while you cook the stone fruit.

Brush the fruit halves with olive oil and season with salt, pepper and thyme leaves. Put them onto the hot area of the grill, cut side down. Do not turn until you've achieved some char lines, as this colour is what will be giving you the flavour (this will take 3–4 minutes). Turn and grill on the other side, just to soften them, for 2 minutes.

Remove everything from the grill and leave it to rest for a few minutes.

Toast the pine nuts in a baking tray over the grill for 2–3 minutes. Keep tossing them, and remove them from the heat as soon as they start to colour.

Tear the burrata over the grilled fruit and drizzle with extra-virgin olive oil. Garnish with the toasted pine nuts, basil and mint. Season with salt and serve on a big plate in the centre of the table.

SMOKEY MEATBALL GRATIN WITH SOURDOUGH TOASTS

Serves 4

Although this is more of a chef's late-night snack than a feast, it's too good not to share. When I hear the phrase 'comfort food', this is what springs to mind. Cook and serve in your most homely dish in the centre of the table with the stack of crispy toasts.

2 tbsp olive oil, plus extra for drizzling
1 large onion, finely diced
2 garlic cloves, crushed, plus 1 garlic clove, peeled and left whole
400g finely ground pork mince
1½ tsp sea salt
½ tsp freshly ground black pepper
1 large egg, beaten
40g ground almonds
15g thyme sprigs, leaves finely chopped
6g rosemary sprigs, leaves finely chopped
2 red peppers, deseeded and cut into quarters
125g mini buffalo mozzarella balls
a few sage leaves
4 thick slices of sourdough bread

FOR THE SAUCE
1 large onion, diced
1 carrot, diced
1 celery stick, diced
2 tbsp olive oil
2 large garlic cloves, finely chopped
1½ × 400g tins chopped tomatoes
1 tsp sea salt
½ tsp freshly ground black pepper
1 tbsp light brown sugar
2 tsp smoked paprika

Preheat the oven to 200°C (180°C fan oven) gas mark 6. Heat the oil in a frying pan over a low heat, add the onion and crushed garlic and cook, stirring regularly, for 20 minutes or until light golden and caramelising.

Put the onion and garlic in a large bowl and add the pork, salt, pepper, egg, almonds and herbs. Mix together until well combined then form the mixture into bite-sized balls.

Drizzle some oil into a roasting tin, add the meatballs and scatter the pepper quarters around them. Drizzle over a bit more oil. Put in the oven and bake for 20 minutes or until golden and cooked through.

Meanwhile, make the sauce. Put the onion, carrot and celery in a saucepan with the oil. Sweat down over a low heat, covered, for 10 minutes or until everything is tender. Add the remaining ingredients and cook for 20 minutes or until thickened and rich.

Pour the sauce over the cooked meatballs and peppers in the roasting tin. Tear the mozzarella over the top and scatter over the sage leaves. Return to the oven for a further 10 minutes or until golden on top.

Meanwhile, make the toasts. Preheat a griddle pan to scorching hot. Cut the whole garlic clove in half and rub the cut surface of the garlic over both sides of each of the bread slices. Drizzle the bread generously with olive oil and place on the griddle. Cook for 4–5 minutes on each side until black lines appear on the bread. Serve with the meatballs and sauce.

172 Dusk

PHEASANT KIEVS

There is always an abundance of pheasant to use up during the autumn and winter months. It's so nice to be able to enjoy this plentiful, free-range meat. Something different from the standard pheasant braise (which can quite repetitive, come February) is always handy to have up your sleeve. These Kievs, oozing with buttery garlic and parsley, make a fantastic family supper.

As pheasant breasts are quite small you should be able to fit four Kievs into one large ovenproof frying pan. This effectively makes this a one-pan supper, ready in under 20 minutes.

Serves 4

4 pheasant breasts, skinned
6 garlic cloves,
    finely chopped
zest of 1 lemon
a large bunch of flat-leaf
    parsley, finely chopped
200g butter, softened
4 tbsp plain flour
2 large eggs, beaten with
    a splash of milk
200g dried breadcrumbs
sunflower oil, for frying

Preheat the oven to 190°C (170°C fan oven) gas mark 5. Start by making a pocket in the thick part of each pheasant breast using a small, sharp knife.

Put the garlic in a mortar and add the lemon zest and parsley. Grind together using a pestle to make a paste, then stir in the softened butter. Using a teaspoon, scoop the butter paste evenly into the pockets of the four pheasant breasts.

Put the flour, eggs and breadcrumbs into three separate mixing bowls. Roll a pheasant breast in the flour, then in the egg and then finally in the breadcrumbs. Repeat the process with the other breasts.

Heat a little oil in an ovenproof frying pan over a medium heat and pan-fry the breasts on one side for 2 minutes. Flip them over and pop the whole pan in the oven to bake for 12 minutes until golden and crispy. Serve immediately.

NEW YEAR'S DAY BEEF BRAISE

What better way to blow away the foggy-headed cobwebs than a wander on the beach, cradling a bowl of hot beef braise and horseradish dumplings? It's become a hut tradition. The most important thing to remember is to properly brown the beef before the other ingredients get added to the pot, otherwise your stew will lack colour and flavour. You can make this the day before serving, if you wish. In fact, with more time for the flavours to develop, it will taste even better the next day.

Serves 4

sunflower oil, for frying
1kg chuck steak, cut into
    3cm cubes
1 onion, sliced
1 heaped tbsp plain flour
250ml full-bodied red wine
200ml beef stock
2 garlic cloves, chopped
2 thyme sprigs
2 bay leaves
350g shallots, peeled and
    left whole
2 rashers of smoked streaky
    bacon, chopped into
    thick slices
100g chestnut
    button mushrooms
sea salt and freshly ground
    black pepper

FOR THE DUMPLINGS
160g self-raising flour,
    plus extra if needed
75g beef suet
25g grated fresh
    horseradish (optional)
2 tsp wholegrain mustard
    (optional)
1 tsp sea salt

Preheat the oven to 160°C (140°C fan oven) gas mark 3. Heat a good glug of oil in a flameproof casserole and brown the beef, a few pieces at a time, over a medium-high heat until a rich, dark colour on all sides. Set the browned meat aside on a plate.

Add the sliced onion to the casserole and cook for 4–5 minutes until lightly browned. Return the meat to the pan with the onion and sprinkle in the flour. Stir and allow it to soak up all the juices, then gradually pour in the wine, stirring, followed by the beef stock.

Add the garlic and herbs, and season with salt and pepper, then bring to the boil, cover and cook in the oven for 2 hours.

Heat 1 tablespoon oil in a frying pan over a medium heat and fry the shallots and bacon to give them a bit of colour. Add to the casserole, followed by the mushrooms. Cover and return to the oven to cook for a further hour.

Meanwhile, make the dumplings. Put the flour in a large mixing bowl and add the suet, horseradish and mustard, if using, and the salt. Slowly add a little water at a time and begin to mix it in with your hands until a dough starts to form. Once you have a soft dough with specks of the suet still visible, stop mixing, as you don't want to overwork it. If it is too sticky, add a little more flour.

Using your hands, roll the dough into 12 small balls. Put them on top of the simmering stew and cook, uncovered, for the last 30 minutes of the cooking time. When the dumplings are fluffy and golden, you are ready to serve.

CHICKEN LENTIL STEW WITH ROSEMARY DUMPLINGS

Adding grated carrot to these dumplings gives them a great colour and slight sweetness that offsets the woody rosemary. The truffle oil in the stew brings everything together. If you can get it, use real truffle oil rather than truffle-flavoured oil. I like white truffle oil, as it is more affordable and has a lovely delicate flavour. Just be careful not to add too much, though, as it can easily become overpowering.

Serves 4

olive oil, for frying
4 chicken leg quarters, with skin
2 onions, roughly chopped
2 fennel bulbs, quartered
4 thyme sprigs
2 garlic cloves, chopped
125ml white wine
100g Puy lentils
1.5 litres chicken stock
125ml double cream
1 tsp white truffle oil
sea salt and freshly ground black pepper

FOR THE DUMPLINGS
125g self-raising flour
50g beef suet
1 tsp finely chopped rosemary leaves
1 large carrot, grated
½ tsp sea salt
¼ tsp freshly ground black pepper

Heat some olive oil in a flameproof casserole or large heavy-based saucepan over a medium-high heat, add the chicken and brown it all over. Remove the chicken and put it to one side.

Put the onions in the casserole and add the fennel, thyme and garlic, then cook over a medium heat for 4 minutes or until the onions and fennel are translucent. Add the wine and simmer to reduce by half.

Add the lentils and stock, then return the chicken to the casserole. Bring to the boil, then season with salt and pepper, cover and simmer over a low heat for 25 minutes or until the chicken is cooked through.

To make the dumplings, put the flour in a bowl and add the suet, rosemary and carrot. Season with the salt and pepper. Add 3–4 tablespoons cold water, as needed, to bring the dough together, using a wooden spoon to mix it. Split the dough into 12 even pieces and roll into balls, then put to one side.

Preheat the oven to 220°C (200°C fan oven) gas mark 7. After the chicken has simmered, add the cream and truffle oil. Pour the contents of the casserole into a high-sided roasting tin. Lay the dumplings in the broth around the chicken. Cook in the oven for 20 minutes or until the dumplings are golden brown.

CRISPY PORK BELLY WITH WHOLE SALT-BAKED CELERIAC

Salt-baked celeriac makes an awesome side dish. At the hut, it's presented whole, ripped apart at the table and served with lashings of butter. The high-heat finish on the pork leaves you with crispy crackling to serve alongside the slow-roasted belly meat, celeriac and white bean cassoulet. This spread makes a great autumnal weekend offering.

Serves 4

1kg boneless pork belly in a single piece, unscored
5 sage leaves
2 onions, unpeeled, halved
sea salt and freshly ground black pepper

FOR THE CELERIAC
1 whole celeriac
a drizzle of sunflower oil
300g sea salt
a large knob of butter
a few sage leaves

FOR THE BEANS
6 baby carrots, halved lengthways
2 fennel bulbs, cut into slim wedges
1 cooking apple, peeled and cut into large chunks
4 garlic cloves, sliced
1 tbsp chopped thyme leaves
2 bay leaves
1 tsp sugar
500ml dry cider (scrumpy)
2 × 400g tins butter beans, drained and rinsed
300ml chicken stock
8 sage leaves, shredded
1 tsp sea salt
1 tsp freshly ground black pepper

Preheat the oven to 160°C (140°C fan oven) gas mark 3. Salt the skin of the pork belly and put some sage leaves on the top. Put the two halved onions in a roasting tin, cut side down, and balance the pork belly piece on top of them. Cook for 2 hours 40 minutes.

Meanwhile, prepare the celeriac. Rub the whole celeriac with oil. Scatter half the salt in a small baking tray, add the celeriac and pour the remaining salt on top. When the pork has been cooking for 1 hour, put the celeriac in to bake for 1 hour 40 minutes, or until tender, and a knife inserted into the celeriac goes in easily.

Take the pork and the celeriac out of the oven and keep the celeriac warm by putting it on a warmed serving plate and covering it with foil or a heatproof bowl. Pour off any fat in the pork roasting tin and reserve it. Crank the oven temperature up as high as it will go, 240°C (220°C fan oven) gas mark 9, and cover the pork skin with 1 teaspoon flaked salt. Roast for 40 minutes more, or until the skin is crisp and bubbling.

While the pork continues to cook, prepare the beans. Heat 2 tablespoons of the reserved cooking fat in a large saucepan and add the carrots. Cook over a medium-high heat until they are beginning to brown and caramelise. Add the fennel and apple, and continue to cook until everything is nicely browned. Add the garlic, thyme, bay leaves and sugar, and cook for another 2 minutes. Add the cider and cook for 5 minutes or until the liquid is reduced by half, then add 1½ tins of the butter beans.

Once the pork is done, take the onions out from under the meat and remove their skins. Add the cooked onions to the bean pan, separating the layers as you go, and cook for a further 5 minutes.

Using a blender, purée the remaining ½ can of butter beans with the stock until smooth, then add it to the pan with the sage, salt and pepper. Heat everything through, stirring gently.

To serve, scrape the salt off the celeriac and crack it open. Put the butter on top, in the centre, crack some pepper over and scatter over the sage leaves. Serve the pork with the celeriac and beans.

THYME CHICKEN WITH LEMON POTATOES

At the hut, we cook this dish on a huge wood-fired rotisserie on the clifftop. Our amazing fabricator made the rotisserie using parts from a traditional parrilla and a Stannah stairlift engine! But don't worry, this is a scaled-down version of the recipe that you can cook at home and still has all the flavour. When making the lemon potatoes, use the roasting juices for the second cook so that you get that lovely juicy chicken flavour through them.

Serves 4

50g sea salt
20g thyme leaves
zest and juice of 4 oranges
6 tbsp olive oil
2 garlic cloves, chopped
2 small chickens, each
    split into halves

**FOR THE LEMON
POTATOES**
8 potatoes (ideally Maris
    Piper), scrubbed,
    unpeeled and cut
    into wedges
3 garlic cloves, crushed
150ml olive oil
juice of 2 lemons
1 tsp dried oregano
1 heaped tsp semolina

Put the salt in a mini blender and add the thyme and orange zest. Blend well. Transfer to a bowl and add the juice of three of the oranges, the oil and garlic. Mix well, then rub this marinade all over the chicken halves and leave to marinate in the fridge for 2 hours or overnight if possible.

To make the lemon potatoes, half-fill a saucepan with cold water and parboil the potato wedges for 6 minutes. Drain in a colander, then return them to the pan and give the pan a shake to roughen the edges of the potatoes. Leave them to steam-dry for a few minutes. Put the garlic in a bowl and add the olive oil, lemon juice, oregano and semolina, then mix well and use to coat the potatoes. Put to one side.

Preheat the oven to 200°C (180°C fan oven) gas mark 6. Prepare and heat up your barbecue, if using, so that the coals are white hot. Cook the marinated chicken halves, skin side down, on the grill rack for 3–4 minutes, or until the skin is starting to colour. Turn over and cook for a further 2 minutes. (Alternatively, if using a griddle pan or frying pan, heat it until hot, then sear the chicken halves on all sides to give them some colour.)

Transfer the chickens to two roasting tins and cook them in the oven for 20 minutes. Place the potato wedges around the chicken halves, then return to the oven for 20 minutes, or until the chicken is cooked through. To test whether it is cooked, pierce the thickest part of the meat with the point of a knife; the juices should run clear and the flesh will be white, not pink.

Squeeze the juice from the remaining orange over the chicken halves, then remove from the roasting tins (saving the juices) and leave them to rest on a plate, covered with a few layers of foil to retain the heat, while you second-cook the potatoes.

Turn up the oven temperature to 240°C (220°C fan oven) gas mark 9 and cook the potatoes for a further 10 minutes or until golden brown and crispy. Serve with the chicken.

Shredded
Pork
Shoulder
with
Fennel
Slaw and
Caraway
Flatbreads

Shredded Pork Shoulder with Fennel Slaw and Caraway Flatbreadss

Slow-roasted pork shoulder with ginger rhubarb compote, fennel slaw and toasted caraway flatbreads. This aromatic feast is great for informal gatherings. You can do most of the prep earlier in the day, with the pork cooking in the oven, smelling amazing, as people arrive.

Serves 8

4 garlic bulbs
2.5kg boned and
    rolled pork shoulder
zest of 1 lemon
olive oil, for drizzling
sea salt and freshly
    ground black pepper

FOR THE FENNEL SLAW
8 fennel bulbs
juice of 4 lemons
300ml olive oil
2 tsp caster sugar
2 tsp wholegrain mustard
1 tsp sea salt
a handful of mint,
    leaves chopped
3 onions, chopped

**FOR THE STICKY
GINGER RHUBARB**
700g rhubarb, cut into
    2cm chunks
70g soft brown sugar
a pinch of ground cinnamon
2cm piece of fresh root
    ginger, peeled and
    grated

Preheat the oven to 160°C (140°C fan oven) gas mark 3. Put the garlic bulbs in a large roasting tin and balance the pork shoulder on top. Sprinkle the pork with a good handful of salt and a good coating of black pepper. Sprinkle the lemon zest over the pork, then douse with a good drizzle of olive oil.

Put a double layer of baking parchment over the pork, then cover the whole tin with foil. Roast in the oven for 4 hours.

To make the fennel slaw, top and tail the fennel, removing the outer layer and saving the green fronds to garnish. Finely chop the fennel into slices and put them in a serving bowl.

In a blender, blitz together all the remaining ingredients to make the dressing. Add to the bowl with the fennel, toss well, then garnish with the chopped fronds. Leave to marinate in the fridge for at least 1 hour.

To make the sticky ginger rhubarb, scatter the rhubarb over a baking tray and cover with the sugar, cinnamon and ginger. Give it a good stir to coat and cook, uncovered, in the oven on the shelf above the pork for 40 minutes. Allow to cool, then transfer to a serving bowl.

**FOR THE CARAWAY
FLATBREADS**
1kg plain flour
1 tsp baking powder
4 tsp fine sea salt
2 tbsp caraway seeds
2 tsp ground cumin
4 tbsp sunflower oil,
    plus extra for greasing

To make the caraway flatbreads, put the flour in a large bowl and stir in the baking powder and salt. Add the caraway and cumin and stir to combine. Gradually add enough water to make a dough that is soft and a bit sticky. Add the sunflower oil and knead for 10 minutes or until the dough is smooth. Transfer the dough to a lightly greased bowl, then cover with a clean tea towel or cling film and leave in a warm place to rest for 30 minutes.

Divide the dough into eight pieces, then form into balls and flatten each ball to about 3mm thick.

Heat a griddle pan or frying pan until hot, then cook each dough round for 1 minute on each side or until lightly charred. Remove from the pan and wrap in a clean tea towel to keep warm.

Once the pork is ready, shred it onto a large plate using two forks. Put the pork on the table with the fennel slaw, sticky ginger rhubarb and the flatbreads and let people assemble their own pork flatbreads as they wish.

DUCK, FIG AND PARSNIP ROAST

This is one of those Sunday roasts that is so sumptuous that you probably won't fancy dessert afterwards. I just love duck and figs – they are such a wonderful combination. Serve with kale for added goodness and colour. The figgy gravy will counteract the bitterness of the dark leaf. And don't hold back on the duck-fat roasted parsnips.

Serves 4

4 onions, halved
4 garlic cloves, peeled but left whole
4 rashers of streaky bacon
8 fresh black figs, halved
1 tbsp olive oil, plus extra for rubbing the duck
4 duck legs, knuckles removed
8 parsnips, peeled, quartered lengthways and woody core removed, cut into even-sized chunks
a small handful of thyme sprigs
250ml red wine
500ml chicken stock
1 tbsp cornflour
1 tbsp wholegrain mustard
flaked sea salt and freshly ground black pepper
steamed and buttered kale, to serve

Preheat the oven to 190°C (170°C fan oven) gas mark 5. Put the onions, cut side down, in a roasting tin, then add the garlic and bacon rashers. Add four of the figs and drizzle everything with the olive oil, then toss to coat. Spread them out over the roasting tin.

Rub the duck legs with a little olive oil and put them on top of the ingredients in the tin. Sprinkle sea salt flakes and a dusting of pepper over everything, then roast in the oven for 1 hour.

Take the roasting tin out of the oven and move the duck legs aside. Remove the onions, garlic, figs and bacon from the roasting tin and put to one side. Add the parsnips to the roasting tin, along with the thyme sprigs. Toss everything together to coat the parsnips with the duck fat, and put the duck legs back on top. Add the remaining figs to the roasting tin and return to the oven for another 30 minutes.

Put the roasted onion, garlic, bacon and figs in a saucepan and add the wine and stock. Using a wooden spoon, muddle the onion mixture in the stock to break it down slightly and release the flavour. Cook for 10 minutes over a medium heat to reduce the mixture a little. Put the cornflour in a small bowl and mix with a little water until runny. Stir the mustard and the cornflour into the mixture in the pan and cook for a few more minutes, stirring regularly, until thickened to the consistency you want. Season to taste with salt and pepper.

Serve the roasted parsnips with the duck legs and roasted figs on top. Pour over the figgy gravy and serve with steamed kale.

189   Dusk

SALT-BAKED LAMB LEG WITH GREEN BEAN CAPER SALAD

Baking in a salt crust seals in the flavour of the lamb and ensures that the meat is constantly basted in salty, rosemary-scented juices. This results in a moist, flavoursome meat that begs for the tart caper salad to accompany it.

Serves 4

600g plain flour, plus
   extra for dusting
6 sprigs rosemary,
   leaves roughly chopped
450g fine sea salt
3 large egg whites
olive oil, for frying
1 half leg of lamb
   on the bone, about 1.2kg
400g small new potatoes,
   sliced lengthways
200g French beans,
   trimmed
160g cherry tomatoes on
   the vine
50g pitted black olives
30g small capers
tarragon leaves and flaked
   sea salt, to garnish

FOR THE DRESSING
zest of 1 lemon and 4 tbsp
   lemon juice
a big handful of tarragon,
   leaves chopped
2 shallots, finely chopped
1 tbsp Dijon mustard
120ml extra-virgin olive oil
sea salt and freshly
   ground black pepper

Put the flour in a large mixing bowl and stir in the rosemary and salt. Add the egg whites and 250–300ml cold water, or enough to make a soft but not sticky dough. Wrap the dough in cling film and chill it in the fridge while you sear the lamb.

Heat a little oil in a large frying pan over a medium-high heat and brown the lamb all over. Remove the lamb from the pan and put it to one side to cool. Preheat the oven to 190°C (170°C fan oven) gas mark 5.

Roll the dough out on a lightly floured work surface to a shape large enough to completely enclose the lamb. Wrap it around the lamb, making sure that there are no cracks. Patch any gaps with dough to seal. Put in a roasting tin and roast in the oven for 1 hour.

In the meantime, make the dressing. Put the lemon zest and tarragon in a mortar, and grind using the pestle to bring out the flavour. Put the shallots in a bowl and add the tarragon paste with the lemon juice and mustard. Mix well to combine, then gradually whisk in the olive oil and season with salt and pepper.

Remove the cooked lamb from the oven and leave it to rest in the crust for 30 minutes.

Meanwhile, cook the potatoes in boiling salted water for 15 minutes or until tender and a knife can be inserted easily. When the potatoes are nearly cooked, put the beans in a covered steamer over the top of the pan and cook for the last 4 minutes of cooking. Drain the potatoes in a colander and return them to the pan, then tip in the cooked beans.

Get a saucepan really hot over a high heat and add a tiny drizzle of oil. Add the cherry tomatoes and cook for 2 minutes or until the skins are starting to blister and blacken.

Mix some of the dressing into the potatoes and beans and add the olives and capers. Tip onto a large serving platter and put the tomatoes around the edge, then season the salad with salt and pepper. Serve the lamb carved into slices with some of the dressing spooned over and sprinkled with a few more tarragon leaves, some sea salt flakes and black pepper. Serve while everything is still warm.

Black and Blue Beef

My roasted beef becomes blackened and smokey on the outside while remaining rare and juicy in the middle. If you have access to an outdoor grill, the blackening is definitely best done outside using a heavy-based iron pan over white-hot coals. If that's not possible, make sure you get your hob as hot as it will go and turn your extractor fan on full blast.

Allow a good amount of time to rest the beef after cooking, as this keeps the juices within the meat, which is key to the finish of this dish. You'll need to head to a butcher to buy your beef, due to the size of cut required. Dry-aged beef would be particularly delicious for this.

Serves 8

4 tbsp sunflower oil
2 rib-eye steaks, boned
  and trimmed, about
  1kg each
8 garlic cloves, unpeeled
  and crushed
2 thyme sprigs
100g butter
sea salt and freshly ground
  black pepper
watercress, to serve

**FOR THE DRESSED
BEETROOT**

4kg raw beetroots,
  unpeeled and leaves
  trimmed to 3cm
4 tbsp extra-virgin olive oil
4 tsp sea salt
2 tsp freshly ground
  black pepper
4 tbsp honey
2 tbsp red wine vinegar

FOR THE SALSA VERDE

2 garlic cloves, peeled
4 tinned anchovy fillets
1 tsp flaked sea salt
3 tbsp chopped
  parsley leaves
1 tbsp chopped
  tarragon leaves
1 tbsp chopped mint leaves
1 tsp Dijon mustard
1 tsp white wine vinegar
100ml extra-virgin olive oil

Preheat the oven to 200°C (180°C fan oven) gas mark 6. To make the dressed beetroot, wrap the beetroots in foil and roast for 90 minutes.

To make the salsa verde, put the garlic, anchovies and salt in a mortar, then pound to a paste using a pestle. Add the herbs and pound into the paste. Mix in the mustard and vinegar, and then gently stir in the oil. Pour into a small jug and put to one side to infuse.

Heat two large frying pans over a high heat and add 2 tablespoons sunflower oil to each. Coat the steaks with a heavy seasoning of salt and pepper. When the oil is smoking hot, put one steak in each pan and cook for 2½ minutes on each side, then 1 minute on the fat edge until very well caramelised all over.

Put the steaks in a roasting tin, scatter over the garlic and thyme and roast in the oven for 18 minutes, turning the steaks over after 9 minutes. Transfer the steaks to a baking tray and add the roasted garlic and thyme, then dot the butter on top of the steaks and leave to rest for 15 minutes, turning halfway through. Discard the thyme and garlic.

Once the beetroots are cooked, peel away the foil, then remove the skins and cut each beetroot into wedges. Place in a bowl and dress with the oil, salt and pepper, honey and vinegar. Serve simply, with the steaks and their resting juices, a plate of the dressed beetroot, some watercress leaves and a little jug of the salsa verde alongside.

196   Dusk

BEEF SHIN RAGÙ

As a cut, it's one of the cheapest to buy, as it takes a while to cook, but if you have the patience you'll be rewarded with the most buttery, melt-in-your-mouth texture.

Anchovies are often caught in shoals off the Cornish coast. Their tiny fillets break down when cooked, offering hidden umami back notes. They are the magic ingredient in this ragù.

Serves 4

450g trimmed beef shin
1 tbsp olive oil
40g butter, plus an extra
    knob of butter
2 carrots, grated
1 celery stick,
    finely chopped
2 onions, finely chopped
3 garlic cloves, crushed
2 bay leaves
3 anchovy fillets (fresh
    or tinned)
1 tbsp tomato purée
1 rosemary sprig
250ml red wine
500ml beef stock
400g pappardelle pasta
sea salt and freshly
    ground black pepper
shaved Parmesan, to serve

FOR THE GREMOLATA
zest and juice of 2 lemons
2 garlic cloves, chopped
a large handful of
    flat-leaf parsley
1 tbsp olive oil
2 anchovy fillets (fresh
    or tinned)

Preheat the oven to 180°C (160°C fan oven) gas mark 4. Rub the beef shin with the olive oil and season it. Heat a flameproof casserole on the hob. Add the beef and cook for 3–4 minutes on each side, until browned. Lift out and put to one side.

Take off the heat and, while the pan is still warm, add the 40g butter and leave it to melt, then add the carrots, celery and onions. Put back over a low heat and cook gently for 5 minutes or until softened. Add the garlic and bay leaves, and cook for a further 5 minutes, stirring occasionally. Now add the anchovies and tomato purée. Stir in and cook for another 1 minute.

Add the rosemary sprig and the wine. Bring to the boil, then reduce to a simmer to cook off the alcohol and release the rosemary oil. Pour in the stock and carefully add the beef shin, pouring in the resting juices. Bring to the boil, then cover the casserole and cook in the oven for 3½ hours or until tender, reducing the temperature to 160°C (140°C fan oven) gas mark 3 after 1 hour.

When the ragù is nearly cooked, start making the gremolata. Put all the ingredients into a blender or food processor and season with pepper, then give it a couple of whizzes to roughly cut and blend together. Transfer to a bowl and set aside.

Cook the pasta in a large saucepan of boiling salted water according to the packet instructions until al dente. Drain and add the knob of butter. Once the beef shin is cooked, carefully lift it out. Discard the bay leaves and rosemary.

Using two forks, shred the succulent meat and return it to the sauce. Taste and adjust the seasoning. Serve spooned over the buttered pappardelle with the gremolata drizzled over and topped with a few shavings of Parmesan.

Sticky Ribs with Creamed Mash, Caraway-Roasted Carrots, Crispy Potato Skins and Gravy

Sticky Ribs with Creamed Mash, Caraway-Roasted Carrots, Crispy Potato Skins and Gravy

Melt-off-the-bone, beer-braised ribs that you can cook indoors in the oven – a winter-night winner. The second roast gives the ribs a sticky, caramelised finish and the cooking gravy left in the pan is amazing served in a jug to pour over the mash.

Don't be tempted to use a bitter ale in this recipe. Counterintuitive as it may feel, a light lager works best for flavour.

Serves 8

2.5kg pork spare ribs
5 tbsp sunflower oil
2 star anise
12 garlic cloves, peeled and
    left whole
2 tbsp sea salt
6 onions, sliced
600ml lager
600ml chicken stock
100g light brown sugar
1 tbsp Worcestershire
    sauce
2 tbsp lemon juice

**FOR THE CARAWAY-
ROASTED CARROTS**
8 carrots, untrimmed
2 tbsp light olive oil
2 tbsp caraway seeds
2 tbsp honey
50g butter
sea salt and freshly ground
    black pepper

Split the ribs if they are in one piece. Put 2 tablespoons of the oil in a large saucepan and add the ribs. Fry them on all sides over a very high heat until they really get some colour on them. You will need to do this in batches so that you don't overcrowd the pan.

Once browned, put all the ribs in a clean saucepan (don't wash the other one yet) and cover them with cold water. Add the star anise, ten of the garlic cloves and the salt, and bring to the boil. Once boiling, skim the scum off the top using a fine-mesh sieve, then turn the heat down and simmer for 30 minutes. Take the ribs out of the pan and spread them out in a roasting tin, then set aside. Preheat the oven to 200°C (180°C fan oven) gas mark 6.

Using the pan you browned the ribs in, add the onions, the remaining two garlic cloves and 3 tablespoons oil. Deglaze the pan with the lager, stirring with a wooden spoon. Add the stock and sugar and simmer for 8–10 minutes or until the liquid has reduced a little. Add the Worcestershire sauce and lemon juice. Pour this gravy, along with the onions, over the pork ribs in the roasting tin. Roast the ribs in the oven for 40 minutes.

Meanwhile, prepare the carrots for roasting. Scrub them well and, if they are quite slender, leave them whole. Otherwise, slice them once lengthways and put them in a wide saucepan

**FOR THE CREAMED MASH
AND CRISPY SKINS**
1.5kg potatoes (ideally
    King Edwards)
olive oil, for drizzling
80g butter
100ml milk
2 tbsp double cream

and cover with cold water. Add some salt and bring to the boil. Simmer for 5 minutes and then drain. Coat the carrots in the olive oil and season with a pinch of salt and pepper. Lay on a roasting tin and roast in the oven with the ribs for 20 minutes.

Next, prep the potatoes. Thickly peel the skins off using a sharp knife, keeping the peels to one side. Cut the potatoes into quarters and boil for 20–25 minutes until tender. Once done, drain in a colander and put to one side in the saucepan.

Once the carrots have had their first roast, take them out for spicing. Lightly crack the caraway seeds using a mortar and pestle and sprinkle over the carrots. Drizzle with honey and dot knobs of the butter over the top. Toss to mix well. Put back in the oven for a further 10 minutes, basting halfway through with the buttery caraway juices to ensure they really pick up the flavour.

Once the ribs have had their 40-minute first roast, take them out of the oven and carefully pour the liquid from the tray into a saucepan. Give the ribs a turn and return to the oven for another 20 minutes to crisp up and caramelise.

When the carrots' second roast is done, take them out of the oven and cover with a couple of layers of kitchen foil to keep warm.

Put the potato skins onto a baking tray with some salt, pepper and oil. Put the tray with the skins on the top shelf of the oven above the ribs and crisp them up until golden. Keep a close eye on them; they usually take about 20 minutes, but it depends on their thickness and the heat of the oven.

Meanwhile, the boiled potatoes should now be nice and steamy. Add the butter, milk, cream and salt and pepper and whip until smooth with an electric beater. Keep the potatoes warm in the pan over a low heat.

Once crisped up, take the ribs out of the oven and use tongs to transfer from the baking tray onto your serving platter. Pour a splash of boiling water into the baking tray to deglaze it. Carefully pour this into the saucepan with the cooking juices. Heat on the hob over a medium-high heat, stir and season with salt and pepper to taste. This is your gravy.

Serve the ribs in a big pile on a platter in the centre of the table with some serving tongs. Add a bowl of the mash, a dish of the carrots, a jug of the cooking gravy and a mounded plate of the salted, crispy skins. Don't forget the roll of kitchen paper for the inevitable sticky fingers!

RAINBOW ROOT TART

Vegetable ribbons make an attractive tart – get creative with their colours and arrangement. It's wise to lightly cook and soften them first, as they will be tricky to handle and keep in place otherwise.

Serves 4

320g ready-rolled
    shortcrust pastry
plain flour, for dusting
1 small carrot
1 small parsnip
1 small courgette
1 large raw beetroot
sunflower oil, for frying
½ large onion, sliced
    lengthways
300g soft, crumbly
    goat's cheese
2 large eggs
50ml double cream
2 tbsp chopped
    oregano leaves
2 tbsp chopped
    thyme leaves
sea salt and freshly
    ground black pepper

On a lightly floured work surface, roll out the pastry sheet a little more until it is large enough to line a 25cm tart tin. Use the pastry to line the tin and prick all over the base with a fork. Trim the edges and chill in the fridge for 30 minutes. Preheat the oven to 210°C (190°C fan oven) gas mark 6½.

Line the pastry case with a sheet of baking parchment and enough baking beans to cover the base. Bake blind for 10 minutes, then remove the paper and the beans, and bake for a further 3–5 minutes until the case is pale golden. Leave to cool.

Meanwhile, cut the carrot, parsnip and courgette into ribbons using a swivel vegetable peeler, keeping the vegetables separate. Use the peeler to make ribbons from the beetroot, too – this is a bit trickier, as you will have to go around the middle of the vegetable.

Heat 1 tablespoon of the oil in a wok or large frying pan and fry the onion for 2 minutes. Add the carrot ribbons and keep cooking until the onion begins to brown and the carrot is softened. Remove from the pan, pour in a little more oil and add the parsnip. Fry until softened, then remove from the pan, add the courgettes and cook to soften. Repeat one more time with the beetroot, keeping this separate or it will make everything pink. Season the cooked veggies with salt and pepper.

Put the goat's cheese in a bowl and add the eggs, cream and herbs, then whisk everything together until well blended. Season well with pepper. Spread this mixture over the tart base.

Pile the vegetables over the cheese filling, making pretty shapes and curls with the ribbons, and popping the beetroot ribbons on carefully at the end rather than tossing them in with the other veg. Bake the tart in the oven for 20 minutes or until it is browning nicely on top, then serve immediately.

205   Dusk

PUMPKIN AND CHESTNUT GNOCCHI WITH CREAMY PORCINI SAUCE

Serves 4

Homemade gnocchi are a real treat and so much more tender than shop-bought. This is a great way to use pumpkin when it is in season. A perfect supper for when the evenings draw in.

1 small pumpkin, peeled, halved and deseeded
olive oil, for brushing
3 potatoes (such as Maris Piper), peeled and quartered
120g peeled cooked chestnuts
2 large egg yolks
freshly grated nutmeg
1 tbsp chopped sage leaves
200g 00 pasta flour, plus extra for dusting
70g dried breadcrumbs
200g butter
sea salt and freshly ground black pepper

FOR THE CREAMY PORCINI SAUCE
20g dried porcini, broken into smallish pieces
40g butter
1 shallot, finely chopped
2 garlic cloves, finely chopped
175ml dry Cornish cider
350ml vegetable stock
2 tsp chopped thyme leaves
60ml double cream

Preheat oven to 190°C (170°C fan oven) gas mark 5. Put the pumpkin halves in a roasting tin and brush with a little olive oil, then sprinkle with salt and roast for 40 minutes. Soak the dried porcini for the sauce in 175ml just-boiled water, then put to one side.

Put the potatoes in a pan of cold salted water and bring to the boil, then cook for 20 minutes or until tender. Mash the pumpkin, potato and the chestnuts until smooth and well combined. Avoid using a food processor or else the mixture will become too gooey. Transfer to a bowl.

Combine the pumpkin mixture with the egg yolks, a grating of whole nutmeg, the sage and a pinch of salt. In a separate bowl, combine the flour and breadcrumbs. Fold this through the vegetable mixture until you have a soft but smooth dough.

Take small spoonfuls of the dough and, with floured hands, roll it into inch-sized pieces. Put to one side while you make the creamy porcini sauce.

Strain the softened porcini, saving the soaking liquid. Melt the butter in a large frying pan over a medium heat and add the shallot, garlic and porcini, then fry for 5 minutes or until softened. Pour in the cider, increase the heat slightly and let the liquid bubble away until it has almost evaporated and there is no smell of alcohol.

Add the stock, the soaking liquid from the mushrooms (leaving any grit in the bottom of the bowl) and the thyme, and simmer for 10 minutes until reduced. Pour in the cream, then season with salt and pepper and warm through. Put to one side.

Bring a saucepan of salted water to the boil and cook the gnocchi for 2 minutes or until they float. Reheat the porcini sauce with a ladleful of the cooking water and swirl the pan to create a creamy sauce. Toss the cooked gnocchi through the sauce and serve.

RED ONION TARTE TATIN

A savoury version of the French classic, this tart looks impressive but is straightforward to make. It's perfect with a rocket salad on the side, and you could even scatter a crumbly goat's cheese over the top.

Serves 4

3 red onions, peeled and
    left whole
50g unsalted butter
1 tbsp light
    muscovado sugar
1 tbsp sherry vinegar
2 tsp chopped thyme leaves
250g puff pastry,
    defrosted if frozen
plain flour, for dusting
sea salt and freshly
    ground black pepper

Preheat the oven to 200°C (180°C fan oven) gas mark 6. Cut each onion into eight wedges, cutting them from root to stem and leaving the root intact so that the wedges hold together.

Melt the butter in a 24cm ovenproof frying pan over a medium-high heat, add the onion wedges and cook for 5 minutes on each side until light golden and softened. Carefully scoop the onions out of the pan using a spatula and put them to one side.

Add the sugar and vinegar to the pan and cook for 2 minutes, stirring, until the mixture caramelises. Remove from the heat and arrange the onion wedges in a circular pattern in the pan, remembering that the tart will be turned out when cooked so that the onion will be on top. Season well with salt and pepper, then scatter the thyme over the top.

Roll out the pastry on a lightly floured work surface and cut it into a circle slightly larger than the pan. Lift the pastry over the onions and tuck in the edges around the onions and down the side of the pan. Make two small slits in the top of the pastry to let out the steam.

Bake in the oven for 25–30 minutes until the pastry is risen and golden. Leave to stand for 5 minutes, then cover the pan with a plate and invert the tart onto the plate – or be brave and quickly slam the tart onto a wooden board to turn it out. Serve warm, cut into wedges.

209   Dusk

Slow-Roasted Goat in Preserved Lemons with Grilled Za'atar Summer Squash and Confit Potatoes

Slow-Roasted Goat in Preserved Lemons with Grilled Za'atar Summer Squash and Confit Potatoes

Goat is becoming an ever more-popular meat. It's a really ethical option in Cornwall, with just a handful of small-scale goat farmers. The meat is similar to lamb, but leaner and more subtle in flavour. It really lends itself to Middle Eastern seasonings, too. Start preparing this dish the night before. If you can't get summer squash easily, just go for courgettes.

Serves 8

2 onions, quartered
1 goat shoulder on the bone, about 2.5kg
8 potatoes (ideally Maris Piper) about 260g each, peeled and cut into 4cm-thick discs
600g goose fat
1 litre sunflower oil
1 garlic bulb
thinly pared strips of zest from 1 lemon
4 rosemary sprigs
1kg summer squash such as patty pan, or courgettes, cut lengthways into 2cm-thick slices
200ml extra-virgin olive oil
800g cherry tomatoes
200g Greek yogurt
a squeeze of lemon juice
1 tbsp honey
sea salt and freshly ground black pepper

Start the night before by making the marinade. Put the seeds in a dry frying pan over a high heat and toast until they just start to crackle. Tip into a food processor and pulse for a few seconds to split the seeds. Add the remaining ingredients and 400ml water, then blitz to make a chunky paste.

Lay the quartered onions over the base of a large roasting dish, ideally earthenware, or a roasting tin, then put the goat shoulder on top and smear the marinade evenly over the surface of the meat. Cover with baking parchment and leave to marinate in the fridge overnight.

You'll want to make the confit potatoes the night before too. Preheat the oven to 120°C (100°C fan oven) gas mark ½. Put the potato slices in a large, deep roasting dish or tin and cover them with the goose fat and oil, making sure they are completely submerged. Add the garlic, lemon zest and rosemary. Roast in the oven for 1 hour and 20 minutes, then remove and leave the potatoes and flavourings in the oil, covered, to infuse overnight.

The next day, about 4 hours before you want to eat, preheat the oven to 240°C (220°C fan oven) gas mark 9 and roast the

2 tbsp coriander seeds
2 tbsp cumin seeds
1 tsp fennel seeds
6 preserved lemons, rinsed
    and roughly chopped
2 tbsp onion powder
2 tbsp garlic powder
2 fennel bulbs,
    roughly chopped
a big bunch of coriander,
    leaves roughly chopped
200ml olive oil
1 tsp sea salt
½ tsp freshly ground
    black pepper

FOR THE ZA'ATAR
2 tbsp sesame seeds
1 garlic clove, crushed
4 tbsp finely chopped
    oregano leaves
2 tsp dried thyme
2 tsp ground sumac
1 tsp lemon zest
250ml extra-virgin olive oil
1 tsp sea salt

goat, uncovered, for 10 minutes at that temperature. This will seal the meat. Take the dish out of the oven, reduce the heat to 170°C (150°C fan oven) gas mark 3½ and cover with baking parchment, then cover again with kitchen foil and wrap tightly. Roast for 4 hours.

Meanwhile, make the za'atar. In a dry frying pan, toast the sesame seeds over a medium heat for 3 minutes or until they begin to brown and get aromatic. Put to one side in a bowl to cool. Once cooled, mix in all the other ingredients and leave to one side until ready to serve.

Once the goat is cooked, take it out of the oven and leave it to rest for 15 minutes. Turn the oven heat up to 240°C (220°C fan oven) gas mark 9. Take your roasting dish of confit potatoes and lift the potatoes out of the oil using a slotted spoon. Put them onto a non-stick baking tray and season with salt and pepper, then cook in the oven for 10–15 minutes until golden.

While the goat is resting, grill the vegetables. For the best flavour cook them over hot coals on a charcoal grill. Otherwise, preheat the grill to its highest setting. Lay out the squash slices on a baking sheet and coat them in two-thirds of the olive oil. Leave them to stand for a few minutes while you coat the tomatoes in the remaining oil. Grill the squash on one side for 4 minutes or until seared and coloured, and then on the other side for 2–3 minutes until nicely charred and smokey but not mushy. Grill the cherry tomatoes for 2–3 minutes until they are lightly charred.

Place the goat in the centre of table with two forks for serving: the meat should easily fall off the bone. Drizzle some of the za'atar mix over the grilled summer squash and tomatoes. Stir 3–4 tablespoons of the za'atar mix, to taste, into the yogurt and add a squeeze of lemon and the honey to make a za'atar yogurt dressing for the goat. Season to taste with salt and pepper. Serve the goat with the confit potatoes, grilled vegetables and za'atar yogurt dressing.

The final treat of the day: pudding. I can't introduce this chapter without a nod to my lovely mother-in-law, Maggie. Coming from a generation of bakers in Portscatho, she was the pioneer of our baking at the hut in the early days and we still use her recipes today. I just had to include some of them here. Anyone who's tried her cakes will know why!

Alongside Maggie's recipes, you'll also find some of my favourite desserts. At home, I only tend to make dessert when we have friends round, so these recipes are all pretty relaxed and great for sharing.

4

Afters

WILD BLACKBERRY AND MINT GRANITA

In September, get your wellies on, grab a pot and head out blackberry picking. If you manage to get home with some uneaten berries in your pot, you've done well! Reward yourself with a delicious and refreshing granita.

Serves 4–6

100g caster sugar
400g blackberries
juice of 1 lemon
20 mint leaves, chopped,
    plus a few very small
    leaves to garnish
Cornish clotted cream,
    to serve (optional)

Put the sugar in a small saucepan with 300ml water and bring to the boil, stirring, until the sugar has dissolved. Reduce the heat and simmer for 4 minutes, then remove from the heat and leave the syrup to cool completely.

Meanwhile, put the blackberries into a food processor with half the lemon juice and blitz to a purée. Add the cooled syrup and blend to combine well. Taste the mixture, and if it is a bit too sweet add the remaining lemon juice, to taste (it will depend on the ripeness of your blackberries). Pass the mixture through a fine sieve to remove the blackberry seeds, then stir in the chopped mint.

Transfer the mixture to a shallow freezerproof container with a lid. Freeze for 2 hours, then remove the container from the freezer and use a fork to break up the mixture, which should just be starting to freeze in places. Return to the freezer for another 1 hour, then repeat, using a fork to stir and break up the ice crystals. Continue to do this for the next 2 hours, stirring once an hour, until the mixture is evenly frozen into small ice crystals.

After this, the mixture should stay as it is and you can keep it in the freezer until you are ready to eat. Scoop the granita into small bowls or glasses and scatter over the mint leaves. Serve with a scoop of clotted cream, if you like.

BROWN BREAD ICE CREAM
WITH WARM CHERRIES

If you've never tried brown bread ice cream before, you're in for a real treat. Make the sauce when cherries are in season and at their sweetest. The hardest thing about it is not eating too many of the cherries as you're removing the stones – 'two for the pot, one for me' is my rule of thumb.

Serves 4

140g wholemeal bread with crusts, roughly torn into pieces
100g muscovado sugar
2 large eggs, separated
1 tbsp dark rum
2 tsp vanilla bean paste
500ml double cream
100ml single cream
100g icing sugar

FOR THE WARM CHERRIES
2 large handfuls of ripe cherries, stones removed
a large knob of butter
2 tbsp caster sugar
1 cinnamon stick
2 tbsp dark rum

To make the brown bread ice cream, preheat the oven to 180°C (160°C fan oven) gas mark 4 and line two baking trays with baking parchment. Blitz the bread in a mini food processor to make coarse crumbs – you don't want the pieces to be too small. Mix together the breadcrumbs and sugar, then tip onto the prepared baking trays and spread out in an even layer.

Toast the crumbs in the oven for 25 minutes, turning them and swapping the trays around halfway through, until the crumbs are dark and caramelised. Leave to cool.

Put the egg whites in a clean, grease-free bowl and whisk until they form stiff peaks. Put the egg yolks in a separate bowl and add the rum and vanilla bean paste, then mix until combined.

In a third bowl, whisk both types of cream with the icing sugar until thickened to soft peaks. Fold the egg yolk mixture into the cream, then gradually fold in the egg whites.

Spoon the mixture into an ice cream maker and churn, following the manufacturer's instructions (you may need to do this in batches). Just before the ice cream is ready, stir in the caramelised breadcrumbs. Spoon the thick and creamy mixture into a freezerproof container with a lid to freeze until firm. (Alternatively, if you don't have an ice cream maker, spoon the mixture into a freezerproof container and freeze for 4 hours, stirring the mixture twice during this time.) Remove from the freezer 20 minutes before serving to soften.

To make the warm cherries, heat a saucepan over a low heat and add the cherries, butter, sugar and cinnamon stick. Heat until the cherries caramelise, then add the rum and remove from the heat. Serve the warm cherries poured over the brown bread ice cream.

ORANGE CARDAMOM CAKE

As the saying goes, good things come to those who wait. It is a slow, although simple, process to prepare the cake, but the result is a sumptuous and fragrant bake that is worth every second of preparation time. This tastes sublime served with a scoop of crème fraîche or chocolate sorbet.

Serves 8

3 whole oranges (ideally blood oranges, if available)
375g ground almonds
375g caster sugar
2 tsp baking powder
9 large eggs
crème fraîche, to serve (optional)

FOR THE SYRUP
juice of 1 orange
juice of ½ lemon
50g granulated sugar
seeds from 4 cardamom pods

TO DECORATE
1 orange (ideally blood orange), peeled, pips removed, sliced into 5mm-thick discs
1 handful of pistachio nuts

Put the oranges in a saucepan over a medium heat and cover with water. Bring to the boil, then reduce the heat, cover with a lid and cook gently for 2½ hours. Remove the oranges, then cut them in half and remove any pips. Put into a blender or food processor and blend until smooth.

Preheat the oven to 180°C (160°C fan oven) gas mark 4 and line a 25.5cm round cake tin with baking parchment. Weigh out 550g of the orange purée and put it in a large mixing bowl. Mix the orange purée with the almonds, sugar and baking powder using an electric beater.

While still mixing, add the eggs, one at a time, until you have a smooth batter. Pour into the prepared cake tin and bake for 45 minutes.

Meanwhile, to make the syrup, put the orange and lemon juice in a saucepan and add the sugar and the cardamom seeds. Cook over a medium heat to dissolve the sugar, and then increase the heat to high. Cook for 5 minutes to reduce the liquid.

Leave the cake in the tin and put on a wire rack, then arrange the orange slices over the top. Pour over the syrup and leave the cake in the tin to cool.

Put the nuts between two sheets of baking parchment and use a rolling pin to crush them roughly. When the cake is cool, turn it out of the tin and sprinkle with the crushed pistachio nuts. Serve with a dollop of crème fraîche, if you like.

STRAWBERRY BAKE

Here is a lovely comforting summer pudding that goes famously with clotted cream. It's a firm staff favourite at the hut, so Maggie bakes one for the counter and one for us.

Serves 6–8

180g butter, softened, plus extra for greasing
180g golden caster sugar
180g self-raising flour
180g ground almonds
1 tsp ground cinnamon
1 large egg, plus 1 large egg yolk
450g fresh strawberries, hulled and sliced
icing sugar, for dusting
Cornish clotted cream, to serve

Preheat the oven to 180°C (160°C fan oven) gas mark 4. Butter and line the base of a 23cm round loose-based cake tin with baking parchment. In a food processor, mix together the butter, sugar, flour, ground almonds, cinnamon, egg and egg yolk, until well combined. (Alternatively, put all the ingredients in a large mixing bowl and use an electric beater or a wooden spoon to mix well.)

Tip half the mixture into the prepared cake tin and smooth the surface. Arrange the strawberries on top and then pour over the remaining cake mixture, so that you have a layer of strawberries in the centre. Spread the surface smooth and bake for 1 hour–1 hour 10 minutes until slightly risen and a rich golden brown. Check after 40 minutes that it's is not getting too brown; if it is, loosely cover with foil.

Leave the cake in the tin to cool for 5 minutes on a wire rack, then remove it from the tin and dust it with icing sugar. Serve warm with clotted cream.

BAKED AND BRULÉED RICE PUDDING

Laced with warming spices and finished with a delicate brûlée topping, this is no ordinary rice pudding. Use the best-quality dairy you can afford and don't be shy with the nutmeg.

Serves 4

½ vanilla pod
500ml whole milk
300ml single cream
120g short-grain
    pudding rice
100g caster sugar
1 cinnamon stick
a pinch of freshly grated
    nutmeg, plus extra
    for sprinkling
2 thinly pared strips of
    orange zest, avoiding
    the white pith

FOR THE BRÛLÉE TOPPING
2 tbsp caster sugar

Preheat the oven to 180°C (160°C fan oven) gas mark 4. Cut the vanilla pod in half lengthways and scrape out the seeds onto a plate. Put the milk in a saucepan and add the cream, rice, sugar, cinnamon stick, vanilla seeds, nutmeg and strips of orange zest. Cook over a medium heat, stirring occasionally, for 5 minutes or until it reaches a simmer. Remove from heat and put to one side for 15 minutes to infuse.

Remove and discard the cinnamon stick. Pour the rice mixture into a 1 litre ovenproof dish. Sprinkle with extra nutmeg, then bake in the oven for 1 hour or until the rice is tender and the custard is set. Remove from the oven and put to one side for 10 minutes.

To make the brûlée topping, evenly sprinkle the sugar over the surface of the pudding. Using a small kitchen blowtorch, torch the sugar until caramelised to create the brûlée finish, or alternatively put the dish under a hot grill and caramelise the top until golden. Serve immediately.

KEA PLUM AND MARZIPAN TART WITH HOMEMADE CLOTTED CREAM

Only found on the banks of the River Fal, Kea plums are something rather special. They are a particularly tart variety of plum that goes beautifully with the soft richness of marzipan. They're very hard to come by outside of the village of Kea, so it's more of a namecheck than a required ingredient. Any small English plum will work well.

Serves 8

225g plain flour, plus extra for dusting
75g caster sugar
115g chilled butter, cut into cubes
3 large egg yolks
100g apricot glaze or jam

FOR THE HOMEMADE CLOTTED CREAM
1 litre unhomogenised full-cream milk (the old-fashioned gold-top stuff, sold as Graham's Family Dairy in major supermarkets)

FOR THE FILLING
80g butter, softened
100g caster sugar
2 large eggs
1 tsp orange extract
80g plain flour
1 tsp baking powder
100g marzipan, cut into 1cm dice
400g small plums, halved and stoned

First make the clotted cream. Pour the milk into a wide heavy-based saucepan and leave to stand, covered, in a cool place overnight. By morning, the fat should have risen to the top. Move with caution so as not to disturb the fat layer.

Heat the pan of milk over a very low temperature for ¾–1 hour without stirring, being very careful not to let it boil, until a thick golden crust starts to form. This is called scalding the milk.

Gently remove the pan from the heat, being careful not to disturb the fat layer, cover and put it back in the cool place. Leave to set for about 12 hours.

By this point, there should be a lovely layer of clotted cream formed on the top, which you can scrape off using a wide-bladed knife, and serve. Retain the skimmed milk to use for drinks or cooking.

To make the pastry, put the flour, sugar and butter in a food processor and blend until you get a breadcrumb texture. (Alternatively, rub the flour and butter together using your fingertips until it resembles breadcrumbs, then stir in the sugar until well combined.) Add the egg yolks and pulse, or stir, until the mixture starts to come together into a dough. Tip out onto a floured work surface and bring it together into a ball of dough.

Wrap in cling film and chill it in the fridge for 30 minutes. Preheat the oven to 200°C (180°C fan oven) gas mark 6.

Roll out the pastry on a lightly floured work surface until it is large enough to line a deep-sided, loose-based 23cm round tart tin. Line the tin, patching up any holes as you go, and trim the edges. Put the lined tin back in the fridge to chill while you make the filling.

Put the butter and sugar in a mixing bowl and whisk until light and fluffy. Add the eggs and orange extract, and whisk again. Sift in the flour and baking powder, then fold in using a spatula until well combined.

Pour this batter into the chilled pastry case and scatter the marzipan dice over the top. Arrange the plum halves, cut side up, over the top of the tart – there will be spaces in between where the batter will bubble up nicely.

Bake the tart in the oven for 40 minutes – check it after 25–30 minutes and cover the top with foil if it is browning too quickly. Test that it is cooked through by inserting a skewer, which should come out clean, then leave it to cool for 10 minutes in the tin on a wire rack.

Meanwhile, put the apricot glaze in a saucepan and heat it gently so that it dissolves. Thin it down with a drop of water, if needed, so that you have a loose, brushing consistency. If you are using jam, pass it through a fine sieve to remove any lumps of fruit.

Turn out the tart and brush the glaze all over the top and sides. Slice into wedges and serve with the clotted cream.

CARAMELISED LEMON TART WITH LAVENDER

Everyone loves a lemon tart, and this one is made even more special by using a toasted-hazelnut pastry, a caramelised brûléed top and finished with a sprinkling of lavender flowers. Make sure you buy edible lavender, which hasn't been sprayed with any chemicals before you use it.

Serves 6–8

FOR THE PASTRY
25g hazelnuts
200g plain flour, plus
    extra for dusting
110g chilled butter,
    cut into cubes
1 large egg, lightly beaten

FOR THE FILLING
4 large eggs, lightly beaten
125g caster sugar
150ml double cream
juice of 4 lemons and the
    zest of 3
icing sugar, for dusting
dried edible lavender
    flowers, plus extra sprigs,
    to decorate

Preheat the oven to 190°C (170°C fan oven) gas mark 5. Spread the hazelnuts over a baking tray and cook in the oven for 7–10 minutes until the skins have darkened and the nuts are golden underneath. Turn off the oven. Rub the nuts between two clean tea towels to loosen the skins. Pick the hazelnuts out from the skins. Leave to cool, then grind them to a powder in a food processor.

To make the pastry, put the flour and butter in a food processor and blend until you get a breadcrumb texture. (Alternatively, rub the flour and butter together using your fingertips until it resembles fine breadcrumbs). Stir in the ground hazelnuts and enough of the egg to make a smooth dough. Wrap the pastry in cling film and chill in the fridge for 15 minutes. Roll out the dough on a lightly floured work surface until it is large enough to line a 23cm round tart tin. Lay the pastry over the tin and press it into the edges and up the side, then prick the base all over with a fork, trim the edges and chill in the fridge for another 15 minutes.

Preheat the oven again to 190°C (170°C fan oven) gas mark 5. Line the pastry case with a piece of baking parchment and add enough baking beans to cover the base. Bake blind for 15 minutes, then remove the paper and beans and return the pastry case to the oven to bake for another 10–15 minutes until light golden.

Continues on next page

Meanwhile, to make the filling, put the eggs in a bowl and add the sugar. Beat together using an electric beater until the mixture leaves a thin ribbon trail when the whisk is lifted. Stir in the cream and lemon juice. Strain the mixture into a jug and stir in the lemon zest.

Turn the oven temperature down to 170°C (150°C fan oven) gas mark 3½. Carefully pour the filling into the pastry case and bake for 30–35 minutes until the filling is set but is still a bit wobbly. Dust the top of the tart with a layer of icing sugar and, with a kitchen blowtorch or in a preheated grill, brown the top until the sugar melts and caramelises. Scatter a few lavender flowers over the top and decorate with a sprig or two of lavender. Serve warm or cold.

229   Afters

CHOCOLATE CHESTNUT TORTE

The chestnuts give a subtle nuttiness and unique texture to this torte. You can cook and peel fresh chestnuts, or simply use a pack of precooked ones, which are ready to use. There is no better way to welcome in the winter months, and it's naturally gluten-free.

Serves 6–8

250g dark chocolate (at least 50% cocoa solids), broken into small chunks
250g butter
2 tbsp dark rum
zest of 2 oranges
250g peeled, cooked chestnuts
250ml milk
4 large eggs, separated
125g light brown sugar
double cream, or clotted cream, to serve

Preheat the oven to 180°C (160°C fan oven) gas mark 4. Line a 20cm round springform cake tin with baking parchment. Put the chocolate in a heatproof bowl and add the butter, rum and orange zest. Set over a saucepan of gently simmering water, making sure that the base of the bowl doesn't touch the water, and leave to melt, stirring regularly.

Put the chestnuts and milk in a saucepan and heat together over a medium heat until tepid, then blitz in a food processor.

Put the egg yolks in a large bowl and whisk with the sugar using an electric beater. Stir into the chocolate mixture. Add the chestnut purée and stir until well combined. Put the egg whites in a clean, grease-free bowl and whisk until they form soft peaks. Carefully fold into the chestnut and chocolate mixture. Put the mixture into the prepared cake tin and bake for 35 minutes or until firm to the touch. Leave to cool in the tin on a wire rack, then release from the tin and serve with a dash of cream.

233   Afters

BUTTERSCOTCH BLONDIES WITH VANILLA GINGER CUSTARD

We find that these simple, buttery, caramel blondies have the perfect density and a lovely paper-thin crinkly top. The fresh ginger adds a warming hit to the light custard and works brilliantly with the butterscotch blondies. You can vary the flavours for the blondies, perhaps adding chocolate chips, Baileys or a little espresso extract.

Makes 12–16

115g unsalted butter, melted
215g soft dark brown sugar
1 large egg, cold
½ tsp vanilla extract
5 drops of coconut extract
a pinch of sea salt
130g self-raising flour
20g pecan nuts, chopped
½ tbsp dulce de leche
vanilla ice cream, to serve

FOR THE VANILLA GINGER CUSTARD
200ml double cream
125ml whole milk
1 vanilla pod,
    split lengthways
5cm piece of fresh
    root ginger, peeled
    and quartered
4 egg yolks
40g caster sugar

Preheat the oven to 200°C (180°C fan oven) gas mark 6 and line a 20cm square traybake or cake tin with baking parchment. Put the melted butter in a bowl and stir in the sugar until blended. Add the egg, vanilla and coconut extract and salt, then stir vigorously until smooth.

When the batter looks well blended, sift in the flour and stir in. Using a wooden spoon or spatula, beat vigorously – you want to see the batter pulling away from the sides of the bowl. Stir in the chopped nuts and the dulce de leche.

Spread the batter evenly in the prepared tin and bake for 20–25 minutes until a skewer inserted into the centre comes out relatively clean. Cool in the tin on a wire rack, then cut into 12–16 squares.

To make the custard, put the cream, milk, vanilla pod and ginger in a small heavy-based saucepan and heat gently over a medium-low heat. Remove from the heat and leave for up to 1 hour to let the flavours infuse the cream.

Gently reheat the cream until it starts to bubble around the edges, then strain it into a jug, saving the vanilla pod and discarding the ginger.

Using an electric beater, whisk together the egg yolks and sugar in a mixing bowl until smooth. Slowly whisk in 75ml of the cream mixture, then gradually add the remainder. Return the cream mixture to the pan. Using a knife, scrape the vanilla seeds into the sauce and heat gently, stirring often, for 3–4 minutes until thickened to the consistency of double cream. Serve the blondies with the custard drizzled over and a scoop of vanilla ice cream.

STICKY TOFFEE APPLE BUNDT CAKE

Maggie's classic apple cake recipe with luscious sticky toffee caramel poured over. This autumnal bundt cake can be enjoyed either as a dessert with vanilla ice cream or as an afternoon treat with a cup of tea.

Serves 10–12

50g butter, melted and
    cooled, plus extra
    for greasing
300g self-raising flour
250g light brown sugar
2 tsp sea salt
140g ground almonds
4 large eggs
80ml sunflower oil
130ml soured cream
2 eating apples, peeled,
    cored and chopped
    into small pieces
2cm piece of fresh root
    ginger, peeled and
    grated
vanilla ice cream, to serve

**FOR THE STICKY
TOFFEE SAUCE**
150g butter
150g muscovado sugar
½ tsp ground cinnamon
120ml double cream

Preheat the oven to 195°C (175°C fan oven) gas mark 5½ and grease a 25.5cm bundt tin. In a large mixing bowl, combine the flour, sugar, salt and ground almonds. Whisk the eggs with the butter, oil and soured cream. Stir the apple pieces and ginger into the egg mixture, then fold this into the dry mixture.

Pour the batter into the prepared bundt tin and bake for 50–55 minutes or until a skewer inserted into the centre comes out clean. Leave the cake to cool in the tin on a wire rack for 5 minutes, then turn it out gently using a rubber spatula or plastic spoon and leave it to cool.

To make the sticky toffee sauce, melt the butter in a saucepan over a medium-low heat. Add the sugar to the butter and heat until dissolved. Add the cinnamon and cream, stir briefly and gently simmer for 5–6 minutes until sooth and silky in consistency. Drizzle over the apple cake and serve with vanilla ice cream.

CHOCOLATE ORANGE CHOUX BALLS WITH SALTED PISTACHIO CRUMB

Serves 10

There are so many fantastic chocolatiers in Cornwall. For these choux balls I like to use Chocolarder 70 per cent dark, which gives the sauce a rich but softer finish than plain cooking chocolate.

170g unsalted butter, plus extra for greasing
50g caster sugar
240g plain flour
a pinch of sea salt
6 large eggs, or as needed, beaten
200g salted pistachio nuts, shells removed

FOR THE WHIPPED CREAM
800ml double cream
60g icing sugar

FOR THE CHOCOLATE ORANGE SAUCE
400g dark chocolate (70% cocoa solids), broken into small chunks
juice and zest of 4 oranges
100g butter
100ml double cream

Preheat the oven to 220°C (200°C fan oven) gas mark 7 and lightly grease a large baking sheet. Put 400ml water into a large saucepan and add the sugar and butter. Heat gently until the butter has melted. Sift the flour and salt into a bowl. Turn up the heat, then quickly add the flour and salt. Remove from the heat and beat the mixture into a smooth paste using a wooden spoon. Once the mixture comes away from the side of the pan, transfer it to a bowl and leave it to cool for 10–15 minutes.

Beat the eggs into the mixture, a little at a time, until it is smooth and glossy and has a soft dropping consistency. I've suggested six eggs, but you might not need all of them to achieve that.

Using a piping bag and a 1cm plain nozzle, pipe this choux mixture into small balls in lines across the prepared baking sheet. Bake for 25–30 minutes or until golden brown – if the choux pastries are too pale they will become soggy when cool. Put the balls on a wire rack to cool. Spread the nuts on a sheet of baking parchment, then cover with a second sheet and bash them with the end of rolling pin.

For the whipped cream, put the cream in a glass or metal bowl, add the icing sugar and whisk until soft peaks form. Put to one side.

To make the chocolate orange sauce, put the chocolate in a heatproof bowl, add the orange juice and zest and the butter. Set over a saucepan of gently simmering water, making sure that the base of the bowl doesn't touch the water, and leave to melt, stirring regularly. Stir in the double cream, then pour into a jug for serving.

Serve as a stack of profiteroles with a jug of the warm chocolate orange sauce, the bowl of whipped cream and the pistachio crumb to sprinkle over the top.

TATAMS BREAD PUDDING

Tatams is our coffee hut on the next cove along from the Hidden Hut. It's where we bake our morning pastries. This lavish take on traditional bread pudding is made using croissants. Fresh croissants are one of those things you need to eat warm and recently out of the oven. By mid-afternoon, if there are any left over from breakfast, they will have lost their crispness. This is a delicious way to avoid wasting them.

Serves 8

8 baked croissants, slightly stale
200ml semi-skimmed milk
200ml double cream
zest of 1 orange
1 vanilla pod
1 handful of dried cranberries
2 large eggs
75g light brown sugar
30g butter, melted
75g white chocolate chips, or white chocolate chopped roughly into 1cm chunks
demerara sugar, for sprinkling

Tear up the croissants and put them in a large mixing bowl. Add the milk, cream, orange zest, vanilla pod and cranberries, then leave them to soak for a minimum of 30 minutes. Remove the vanilla pod. Beat the mixture with a wooden spoon to ensure the croissant pieces have evenly absorbed the fragrant milk mixture.

Preheat the oven to 180°C (160°C fan oven) gas mark 4 and line a 20cm square cake tin with baking parchment.

Crack the eggs into a bowl and add the sugar and melted butter. Whisk together, then stir into the milky croissant mix. Add the chocolate and stir well.

Pour the mix into the prepared cake tin and sprinkle with demerara sugar to give it a crunchy top. Bake in the oven for 30 minutes, then increase the heat to 200°C (180°C fan oven) gas mark 6 and bake for another 10 minutes or until browned and set. Cool in the tin on a wire rack, then cut into eight portions.

239   Afters

CHOCOLATE ESPRESSO POTS WITH HONEYCOMB

These dark, rich pots, topped with homemade honeycomb, are a great compromise between coffee and dessert. They are ideal for when you have friends over, as they can be prepared the day before and kept in the fridge. Just hide them away from children near bedtime…

Serves 6

225g dark chocolate (70% cocoa solids), broken into small chunks
50ml espresso coffee, or just strong black coffee if you can't do espresso at home
50ml hazelnut liqueur, such as Frangelico
250ml double cream
½ tbsp caster sugar
a pinch of sea salt

FOR THE HONEYCOMB
200g caster sugar
3 tbsp honey
1 tbsp liquid glucose
¾ tsp bicarbonate of soda

FOR THE CREAM TOPPING
150ml double cream
2 tbsp caster sugar

Put the chocolate in a heatproof bowl and add the coffee and hazelnut liqueur, then set aside. In a saucepan, bring the double cream, sugar and salt to the boil. When the sugar has dissolved, pour the hot cream over the chocolate mixture and stir until the chocolate has melted and the mixture is smooth. Divide the mix between six glasses or coffee cups and leave to set overnight in the fridge.

To make the honeycomb, line a baking tray with baking parchment. Put the sugar, honey, glucose and 50ml water in a heavy-based saucepan. Heat through over a low heat until the sugar has dissolved – do not stir – then turn the heat up to high. Allow the mixture to bubble until a deep golden colour and measuring 160°C on a sugar thermometer.

Remove from the heat and leave to stand for 10 seconds, then quickly whisk in the bicarbonate of soda. Immediately pour onto the prepared baking tray and leave to cool for 30 minutes at room temperature (don't put it in the fridge).

Once cooled, break the honeycomb up into shards. To serve, make the cream topping by whipping the double cream with the caster sugar until it just holds its shape. Spoon the cream onto the chocolate pots and serve with shards of the honeycomb on top.

242   Afters

GINGERBREAD TREACLE TART

Add some Cornish fairing biscuits to this treacle filling mix to get lovely gingery notes coming through. I also like to add ground hazelnuts to the mixture for the pastry case – I find the nuttiness balances the sweetness of the filling.

Serves 8

25g roasted hazelnuts
110g salted chilled butter,
    cut into cubes
200g plain flour, plus
    extra for dusting
1 large egg, beaten
100g Cornish fairings
700g golden syrup
200g breadcrumbs, made
    from day-old bread
a pinch of ground ginger
zest of 2 lemons and
    the juice of 1 lemon
Cornish clotted cream,
    to serve

Preheat the oven to 190°C (170°C fan oven) gas mark 5. Spread the hazelnuts over a baking tray and cook in the oven for 7–10 minutes until the skins have darkened and the nuts are golden underneath. Rub the nuts between two clean tea towels to loosen the skins. Pick the hazelnuts out from the skins and leave to cool. Turn off the oven.

Blitz the hazelnuts in a food processor until they resemble a rough flour. Add the butter and plain flour and blitz until the mixture resembles breadcrumbs. Pour into a bowl, then stir in the egg and form the mixture into a dough.

On a floured work surface roll out the pastry and use it to line a 23cm loose-based round cake tin or flan tin, then leave it to rest in the fridge for 30 minutes. Reheat the oven to 190°C (170°C fan oven) gas mark 5.

Prick the pastry base with a fork, then line it with baking parchment and fill it with baking beans. Bake the pastry for 10 minutes. Remove the beans and parchment, then bake for a further 10 minutes.

Meanwhile, put the Cornish fairings into a food processor and blend to a powder. Tip into a large bowl and add the remaining ingredients. Mix until evenly combined so that the breadcrumbs and fairings soak up the golden syrup. Once the pastry is ready, pour the treacle filling into the baked tart case and bake for 30 minutes or until set. Serve warm or cold with a dollop of clotted cream.

245   Afters

RHUBARB AND CUSTARD PAVLOVA

The classic English combo, rhubarb and custard, is even more amazing when served on a bed of fluffy meringue. The meringue does tend to hog your oven for quite a while as it cooks, but it keeps really well – up to 2 weeks in an airtight container – so you can make it well in advance.

Serves 4–6

6 large egg whites
300g caster sugar
a pinch of sea salt

FOR THE CUSTARD
5 large egg yolks
2 tsp golden caster sugar
2 tsp cornflour
800ml double cream
1 vanilla pod

FOR THE RHUBARB
500g rhubarb, trimmed
    and cut into 4cm chunks
50g caster sugar
zest of 1 orange

**FOR THE CRUMBLE
TOPPING**
50g plain flour
30g butter, cut
    into small pieces
25g caster sugar
30g pistachio nuts

Preheat the oven to 170°C (150°C fan oven) gas mark 3 and line a baking tray with baking parchment. Put the egg whites in a large clean, grease-free bowl and use an electric beater to whisk on a medium speed until they start to form nice firm peaks. Whisking on the highest speed setting, gradually add the sugar, spoonful by spoonful, and the salt. Keep whisking until the meringue is glossy and smooth.

Spoon the mixture onto the prepared baking tray to create a large circle, or whatever shape you wish your pavlova to be. Put it into the oven and immediately turn the temperature down to 160°C (140°C fan oven) gas mark 3, then bake for 1 hour or until the meringue looks slightly golden and is fluffy in the middle. Turn the oven off, but leave the meringue inside to cool, ideally overnight but for at least 3 hours.

To make the custard, whisk the egg yolks, sugar and cornflour together in a heatproof bowl. Heat 600ml of the double cream and whole vanilla pod in a saucepan over a medium heat until almost boiling, then remove the pod. Pour this over the egg yolk mixture, whisking constantly.

Wash the pan with cold water and return the mixture to the pan. Cook over a low heat, whisking continuously, for 5 minutes or until thickened. Remove from the heat and cover the surface of the custard with cling film to prevent a skin from forming, then leave it to cool.

Continues on next page

To make the rhubarb, preheat the oven to 200°C (180°C fan oven) gas mark 6. Put the rhubarb in a bowl and add the sugar and orange zest. Mix well, then tip out onto a baking tray. Cook in the oven for 30 minutes or until soft, then leave to cool. Leave the oven on.

To make the crumble topping, line a baking tray with baking parchment. Put the flour and butter in a large bowl and rub them together using your fingertips until they resemble breadcrumbs. (This can easily be done in a food processor if you have one.) Stir in the sugar and spread the mixture out on the prepared baking tray. Bake for 10 minutes or until the crumbs start to turn golden.

Meanwhile, crush the pistachio nuts using a rolling pin, or blitz them in a food processor, to make a rough crumb. Add the pistachio nuts to the crumble mix and give everything a stir, then cook for a further 2–4 minutes until golden. Watch the crumble mix carefully, as you don't want it to burn.

When you are ready to serve, whip the remaining double cream until soft peaks form, then fold it gently into the cooled custard until the mixture holds its shape. Spoon onto the pavlova and spoon the rhubarb on top of the custard cream, drizzling over the cooking syrup. Sprinkle the pistachio crumble on top and serve immediately.

CAMPFIRE FUDGE FONDUE

The kids will love this – as will the adults! The indulgently creamy fudge sauce can be made at home and transported in a flask, if serving it at a barbecue or picnic, so that it stays warm. It can also be left to cool and thicken in the fridge and spread on scones instead of jam. For a salted caramel sauce, add a large pinch or two of sea salt flakes.

Serves 4

150g soft light brown sugar
80g unsalted butter, cubed
300ml double cream
1 tsp vanilla bean paste

SERVING IDEAS
barbecued or chargrilled
    fruit skewers
wedges of pineapple
thick slices of nectarine
    or peach
toasted marshmallows
bananas baked in
    their skins

Put the sugar and butter in a small saucepan and melt gently over a medium-low heat, stirring occasionally. Increase the heat and let it bubble away for a minute or so until starting to caramelise. Stir in the cream and vanilla bean paste and cook for 2–3 minutes until thickened. Remove from the heat and transfer this fudge sauce to a flask, if you like.

To serve, pour the sauce into a bowl and dunk in pieces of barbecued or fresh fruit or toasted marshmallows. Alternatively, slice baked bananas in their skins down the middle and spoon the sauce over the bananas inside.

INDEX

ACKNOWLEDGEMENTS

When embarking on this project, I had no idea of the time and labour that is involved in producing a cookbook. There are so many amazing people who have helped, encouraged and contributed along the way. This single page at the back doesn't really feel like it does you all justice, but here goes...

Kate and the Elton family for coming to a feast night and thinking 'there's a book in this'!

HarperCollins Nonfiction – Katya Shipster, Georgina Atsiaris, James Empringham, Claire Ward, Tom Dunstan, Anna Derkacz, Julie MacBrayne, Isabel Prodger, Jasmine Gordon, Sabrina Yam, Dean Russell – thank you for allowing us this incredible opportunity. Your never-ending patience, positivity and support has been invaluable in seeing this book through to completion. I couldn't have asked for a better team to work with.

Lucy Sykes-Thompson for your vision and creativity that shines through the book from cover to cover.

Grace Cheetham for taking us under your wing and for all your trips down to Cornwall to keep us on the straight and narrow!

Susan Bell and assistants Facundo Bustamante and Anita Barratt – where do I begin? Not every photographer abseils down cliff faces at 5am in the morning for a mussel foraging shot. I feel so privileged to have had you as our food photographer.

Sally Mitchell – for capturing our feast nights so brilliantly and subtly, week in week out, whatever the weather. You and your Nikon have become a much-loved part of our team.

Becks Wilkinson and Katy Aicken, for cooking and styling our recipes into plates of beauty for the camera, through wind, rain and shine.

Olivia Wardle for your boxes and boxes of beautiful, carefully selected props.

Nicky Graimes, Becci Woods and Jan Cutler for your recipe wisdom and amazing attention to detail.

The incredible Cornish artisan growers and producers who supply us on a daily basis and helped source and handpick ingredients for the photoshoots, particularly the Taffinder Family at Curgurrell Farm Shop.

Robin 'Copper' Edwards – for building all of our grills that make our wood-fired feasts possible.

Our amazing hut crew – Dan, Lee, Howard, Alberto, Sarah, Jen, Nik, Frankie and Ceri. Without you none of this would be able to happen. I can't tell you how much I appreciate the constant extra miles you guys put in. Thank you in particular to Dan for your help with the recipe testing and re-testing, and Sarah for holding the fort when Jem and I were working on the book.

Maggie, for your amazing baking knowledge and being a super nan to Oscar when we needed time to write.

Oscar, our wonderful lad who always makes us laugh. Plus, bump on the way. Everything I do is for you two.

And lastly, but not least, my dearest Jem for all her hard work and help with this book. This book or the hut would have never have happened without you. Thank you isn't nearly enough x

Unless otherwise specified in the recipe, all eggs are medium free-range and
all butter is unsalted.

HarperCollins*Publishers*
1 London Bridge Street,
London, SE1 9GF

www.harpercollins.co.uk

First published by HarperCollins*Publishers* 2018

Text © Simon Stallard, 2018
Photography © Susan Bell, 2018 with the exception of pages 6–7, 11, 12–13, 45,
69, 108, 149, 150–151, 166–167, 179, 239, 253 © Sally Mitchell, 2018

10 9 8 7 6 5 4 3 2 1

A catalogue record of this book is available from the British Library.

ISBN: 978-0-00-821801-0

Food styling: Becks Wilkinson
Prop styling: Olivia Wardle

Printed and bound in China

MIX
Paper from
responsible sources
FSC C007454

FSC™ is a non-profit international organisation established to promote the
responsible management of the world's forests. Products carrying the FSC
label are independently certified to assure consumers that they come from
forests that are managed to meet the social, economic and ecological needs
of present and future generations, and other controlled sources.

Find out more about HarperCollins and the environment at
www.harpercollins.co.uk/green